DOMESTIC PARTNERSHIPS IN CALIFORNIA

I do

... don't I?

A GUIDE TO UNDERSTANDING
THE CALIFORNIA DOMESTIC PARTNER
RIGHTS AND RESPONSIBILITIES ACT
FOR COUPLES AND PROFESSIONALS

Mary Kearny Stroube, M.S., J.D.

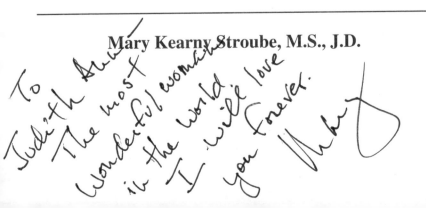

To Judith Ann / The most wonderful woman in the world. I will love you forever. Mary

Published by
Wit's End Press
Woodland, California
United States of America
www.witsendpress.biz
WitsEndPress@AOL.com

Edited by
Britt Alkire

Printed by
Commerce Printing Services
Sacramento, California

Library of Congress Control Number: 2004195776

ISBN 0-9765008-0-9

This book is intended to provide accurate and up-to-date information with regard to domestic partnerships in California. This book is not intended by the author or the publisher to be legal, tax, financial or accounting advice for the reader. It is intended to help a reader formulate questions and be more knowledgeable when seeking professional advice and services.

Neither the author nor the publisher assume any liability for any omission or error in the accuracy of the contents of this book.

For my father.

You would have been proud.

Contents

Appendices

Preface

Each time someone asked about the new domestic partner laws in California, I'd think, "I really should write a book." When friends and colleagues have asked me about it, I'd think again, "I really *should* write that book!" Well, I've done it now. After months of rattling around in my head in its formative stages, it has taken shape.

The most difficult task in writing and organizing this book has been finding the right balance in presenting it so that it can be helpful to the broadest number of people. Foremost, this is for gays and lesbians in California who are considering becoming domestic partners or presently are registered domestic partners. The laws as of January 1, 2005, have the practical effect of suddenly conferring a marital-like status on all who are registered. It is necessary to give serious consideration to the implications of becoming domestic partners. The relationship confers many of the same rights and responsibilities as marriage, although without the benefits that come only come from related federal laws.

While many in the gay community have long wanted marriage or civil unions, now that they are here, everyone needs to understand fully what this means. It will be interesting to see what effects these new laws have on the gay community. Originally, a same-sex couple could register as domestic partners and have the right to visit each other in the hospital or to share a partner's health benefits. Yet suddenly, almost magically, registered domestic partners awakened on January 1, 2005, with new rights and responsibilities that relate to the ownership of property, obligations for debts, the custody and support of children, support of one's partner, estate and inheritance rights and rights for accessing the courts.

This book is also intended for professionals and businesspeople such as clergy, nurses, doctors, all types of therapists and counselors, home contractors, car dealers, real estate agents, bankers and salespeople. Anyone who offers services to the public or has a contractual relationship with a client or customer or patient will want to know about AB 205 and the domestic partner law. This book will likely be an easy read for judges and attorneys, at least from the legal standpoint, although figuring how to manage the limitations of the law will still require considerable creativity and thought.

The law effective January 1, 2005, also applies to opposite-sex couples, at least one of whom is 62 years old and meets the eligibility criteria under Title II of the Social Security Act as defined in 42 U.S.C. Section 402(a) for old-age insurance benefits or Title XVI of the Social Security Act as defined in 42 U.S.C. Section 1381 for aged individuals. I have deliberately not made these domestic partners the focus of this book for two reasons: as heterosexual couples, they are probably more familiar with the legal concepts made applicable by AB 205, and they do not face the added social stigma that accompanies being gay. The legal rights and responsibilities described in the book apply equally to these opposite-sex domestic partners, and professionals and businesspeople need to remember that such couples exist and will be entitled to the same level of service and care under the new laws. While we know that over 25,000 domestic couples have registered in California, the Secretary of State's registration forms do not have a means to distinguish which couples are same-sex and which are opposite-sex.

I have written this book because I believe that all of us should understand our legal rights and responsibilities and make informed decisions. Without enough knowledge, anyone can become entangled in legal situations with significant expenses and with serious potential consequences. It is not my goal to turn everyone into law students, nor do readers need a legal background to read this book. I hope, though, that those of you who read this book will cut me a little slack: I am an attorney, and sometimes, in spite of my best intentions, I just write like an attorney. I've tried to make this book clear and informative. Typical of my style, I seldom do anything without an occasional dash of humor. I know my biases show through, for example, in the belief that gays will always be separate and not equal unless they are allowed to marry and allowed to have access to the accompanying federal rights. I have tried, however, to provide as factual a discussion of the law and its implications as I am able so that all of us can be good consumers of these new rights.

Acknowledgments

When I sat down to write this section, I was amazed to realize the number of people who helped me with this book, many with active reading and critiquing and others with encouragement and enthusiasm. I am blessed with so many good and supportive family members, friends and colleagues.

Britt Alkire is my "partner in crime" in so many pursuits, my gentle editor and writing coach, and the one who kept the coffee and encouragement coming as I sat before the computer working on this book. Each of her readings of the drafts made the book better. I'm not sure I would have finished this project without her support. She also dealt with prospective printers and handled numerous other business matters. My *favorite* sister, even though she is my *only* sibling, Laura S. Hughes, helped proofread and critique the manuscript and handled much of the groundwork getting this book published. I cannot adequately convey my love and appreciation to the two of them.

The Reverend Elder Dr. Freda Smith of Metropolitan Community Church in Sacramento gave me her enthusiastic support and blessing. When Freda says you can do something, it's a done deal! Thank you, Freda.

A number of other friends read the manuscript at various times and gave helpful feedback. Betty (Hornbostel) Wegener, the former chair of the Yolo County chapter of Parents and Friends of Lesbians and Gays (PFLAG) was very helpful both with the content and with her fine-honed copy editing. Her husband Bud provided loving encouragement. Friends and kindred souls Louise Pryor and Nick Charles also took the time to read and to give feedback. My friends Galen Stout, Miles Whitley and Dr. Janet Hause each read drafts and gave me their perspectives. Special thanks to my dear, long-time friend Dr. Satsuki Ina for her careful reading of the book for content and flow. Attorney Nan Goodart took the time to go through the manuscript with particular attention to the estate planning chapter. I feel so much better having had your careful reviews of my work. I'm grateful to you all.

Jon Snellstrom and the Rev. Charles Cooper provided *on-demand* artistic energy. Jon took my typed title page and made a cover design that made this look like, well ... a book! Charles took the cover photo and made me look like, well ... an author!

Other friends and colleagues served as my cheering section and offered many good suggestions for marketing and promotion. My thanks to Marsha Nohl, Maureen McCaustland, Bob Hawke and Dr. Lynne Journey for the support they gave either in reading the drafts or providing ideas for this project. You each made this process easier and the book better. Special acknowledgment is due for my stepmother, Rosalie Stroube, who always thinks I can do anything and will be happy to tell you that anytime.

Writing this book was both harder and easier than I anticipated. The hard part was giving enough information without overwhelming a reader while making sure, at the same time, that the information was accurate. In many ways, the easy part was the actual writing, even through long hours, because I knew this important information must be shared.

Mary K. Stroube
Woodland, CA
December 27, 2004

Chapter 1

Marriage: What's in a Word?

Imagine the scenario: the California Legislature passes new laws that substantially change the divorce[1] laws. Property rights and custody rights would be changed significantly. Even the divorce process itself would change. At an association meeting of all the county clerks, a decision ends the new business agenda: each clerk shall send a letter to every couple married in that county's jurisdiction telling the couple that those "who do not wish to be subject to these new rights and responsibilities MUST terminate..." their marital relationship before the new laws come into effect.[2]

What would happen? Would there be a line at the courthouse the next week with married heterosexual couples starting the divorce process? Would couples hurry to attorneys to learn what the new laws mean for them? Would legal documents be drawn up in an effort to minimize or thwart the intent of the new laws?

Just as important is this particular question: how would all of those couples feel? Would there be a sudden flurry of conversations among couples as they assessed whether it was legally and financially practical for them to remain married? Would they conclude that they took vows "for better or for worse"

---

[1] In California, termination of the marriage is by *dissolution*. As tempting as it is for some people to fantasize *dissolving* their former spouses, I will use the colloquial term "divorce" since that is the term we use in everyday language.

[2] Letter from Secretary of State Kevin Shelley to registered domestic partners on June 4, 2004.

so they had to take whatever came, including changes in the law? Would they be offended that governmental officials thought their marriage vows were so disposable that they would divorce in response to new law?

In June 2004, the California Secretary of State sent out letters to all registered domestic partners[3] in California saying the same thing: the law changes on January 1, 2005, so if you do not want to be subject to the new laws, you must terminate your domestic partnership before the end of the year. The Secretary of State even provided information on the process for terminating the partnership.

In fairness to the Secretary of State, his letter and its contents were dictated by law. In fact, he was required to send out three such notices before January 31, 2005. The laws that go into effect on January 1, 2005 are a major change. What will these new rights and responsibilities mean in everyday terms? How will attorneys and accountants, financial advisers and other professionals need to counsel their same-sex clients? Many same-sex couples have not been married or divorced and will not be aware of the ways in which their rights and responsibilities will change overnight on January 1, 2005. Is there cause for celebration? Have we begun a confounding journey?

California's new laws regarding domestic partners approximate the marriage rights of heterosexual couples within the state. Property rights, the right to support, child custody laws and inheritance rights, among others, change strikingly. The irony of the change is that the process to obtain these rights was, and remains, so simple: complete a one-page form with the name

---

[3] Throughout this book, reference to domestic partners will mean those who are *registered* as domestic partners with the Secretary of State's office. Two types of couples qualify to register as domestic partners in California: 1) two adults of the opposite sex, at least one of whom is 62 years of age or older and meets eligibility requirements for Social Security or Supplemental Security benefits or 2) two adults of the same gender. Domestic partner registration offered by local governments does not provide the same scope of benefits available for state-registered domestic partners.

and address of both parties, have the signatures notarized and take or send the form to the Secretary of State's office along with a minimal fee.

As of January 1, 2005, however, the legal rights and responsibilities of same-sex, registered domestic partners are not so simple. This book is written as a guide for those couples and for the professionals and businesses who advise and serve them. Perhaps most Californians need a good, basic understanding of the new law. As it is with all books about laws, not every question can be answered, and all of the variables that make one couple's situation distinct from that of another's cannot be anticipated. This book should be understood to be a starting point for those wanting to know about the rights and responsibilities of domestic partners in California. Individuals should seek the advice of professionals for answers to questions beyond the scope of this book or in tandem with this book. If the professionals are unsure, they need to find informative education for themselves and do the important research that will be required. The law concerning domestic partners in California will affect hundreds of thousands of people directly.[4]

For years, many well-meaning heterosexuals have expressed their acceptance of gay and lesbian couples by assuming that the lives of gay[5] persons are just like their own

---

[4] The number of people who are gay or lesbian has never been identified. Part of the difficulty in gathering data is due to fear that gays and lesbians have about revealing themselves, and part of it has to do with definitions. The famous researcher Alfred Kinsey used behavior as the basis for his definitions. More contemporary researchers include affectional preferences and self-identification in defining who is homosexual. Still others look for a deeper expression such as an overriding desire for sexual connection or for a pair bond. Gay organizations have typically concluded that about 10% of the population is gay and lesbian. Other researchers put the numbers around 5% and some down around 1-3%. With a population of more than 35 million residents in California, the number of citizens potentially affected may be as few as 350,000 and as many as 3.5 million.

[5] From an inclusive standpoint, the gay and lesbian community usually includes bisexuals and transgendered people. This book is limited to the rights between same-sex domestic partners only. Also, for the sake of

lives except that gay individuals have a partner of the same gender. While in a two-dimensional view, this is true, and the effort to understand and accept is commendable, in practice, no gay couple's life is like that of a heterosexual couple for many reasons: for gays, the laws vary, public acceptance varies, individuals often hold varying religious and moral beliefs about gays which affect the manner in which these same individuals regard gay people or the degree to which they value gay people. *Heterosexism* is a type of prejudice that sets gays apart. Heterosexism is based on societal values that create an assumption that everyone is, or should be, heterosexual. Intentionally or unintentionally, our society gives privileges to heterosexual persons, and devalues, mistreats, or discriminates against lesbians and gays. In its most benign form, heterosexism would assume that a heterosexual's life is the same as a gay person's, simplifying the difference as the gender of one's sexual partners without acknowledging all the ways in which the gay person's everyday life may differ. The presumption is not that both sexual orientations occur normally but rather that heterosexuality is the norm against which gay people should be measured.

Gay people themselves may have a type of internalized homophobia which affects their success and their level of functioning in the world. Although the term *homophobia* has traditionally been used to describe people who dislike or hate gays, the response of these individuals is not truly phobic. Some contemporary authors have used the term *homo-prejudice* or *homo-hatred* to more accurately describe the behaviors. In practice, because gay people are raised in a predominantly heterosexual society and because they often do not recognize until their later teenage or adult years that they are homosexual, many gay people have learned or internalized some of the same societal beliefs about gay people that their families and the larger

---

readability, the term "gay" will be used collectively to refer to both gay men and lesbian women.

society have learned: that gays are characterized as an abomination in the eyes of God and therefore as unworthy or even evil, that gays have a choice about their sexual orientation, that people are gay because of some sort of mental illness or incomplete emotional development or that gay people can never live a fulfilled and fulfilling life. Beliefs such as these can negatively affect one's sense of worth and worthiness and can make it easy for gays to settle for less than their heterosexual counterparts.

Professionals dealing with the new domestic partner laws need to be aware of these differences as gays exercise their new rights and responsibilities. It will be interesting to see how well California courts adapt to the gay couples who will now appear before them in the exercise of these rights and responsibilities. It will be significant to discover if judges can avoid the temptation to treat gay couples just like heterosexually married couples. Although many of the rights for domestic partners in California will parallel the rights of heterosexual couples, the legal situations and predicaments of gay couples will be different, and the implications of various decisions will be different. Nonetheless, federal laws still do not recognize same-sex relationships, and the rights of gay couples will and do have nuances and complexities that many courts may not recognize: a decision that might be made routinely for a heterosexual couple may have adverse federal tax consequences if that same decision is applied to a gay couple. As an example, if a court orders one domestic partner to transfer her ownership interest in a home to the other partner as part of a property settlement, because federal tax laws do not apply to unmarried couples, it is possible that the transfer could be considered a taxable gift with financial consequences for the transferring party.

Depending on whose voice is heard, marriage is either an institution under attack by gays, an institution that is outmoded, a sacrament or simply a legal contract. Marriage is a legal contract, but it is the meaning and the rituals that we have associated with marriage that make the issue of gay marriage so volatile. In polls and surveys, most heterosexual respondents will agree that gay couples should have the right to inherit from each other, should be able to visit each other in the hospital and make medical decisions for each other, and should be able to have custody of their children. However, when asked about marriage for gays, greater than half of those same respondents were strongly opposed. In a national Gallup Poll in May 2003, 49% favored and 49% opposed civil unions for same-sex couples, but 62% favored giving gay couples health care benefits and Social Security survivor benefits. A poll conducted by *The Miami Herald* and *St. Petersburg Times* in March 2004 found that 65% of Floridians oppose same-sex marriage, while 27% are supportive and 8% are undecided. A majority, however, believe that same-sex couples should have equal rights as married heterosexual couples have. Only 41% are supportive of President Bush's push for a constitutional ban on same-sex marriage.

Socially and religiously, we have, as a nation, imbued the concept of marriage with certain meanings that still prevent a broad acceptance of gay relationships *per se* and thereby challenge the idea of marriage for same-sex couples. Some of our religious and political leaders even claim that the institution of marriage is under attack by gays and may not survive if same-sex couples are allowed to marry.[6]

Marriage as a Social Construct

A thorough history of the concept of marriage deserves much more scholarship and detail than is appropriate or necessary for this book. However, the fluid and evolving nature

---

[6] In response to the idea that heterosexual marriages will suffer if the right to marry is extended to gay couples, Massachusetts Congressman Barney Frank humorously mocks such rhetoric by telling how he envisions thousands of husbands waking up the morning after gay marriages are legalized, sitting bolt upright in bed, smacking themselves in the middle of the forehead in the manner of a V-8 Juice commercial and crying out, "Wow! I could have had a man."

of marriage provides a backdrop against which to view domestic partnerships.

Marriage in this age is often about church weddings, women in beautiful white gowns and men in tuxedos. The wedding of Princess Diana and Prince Charles epitomized the dreams of many young women and young men. Rarely do two people sit down to have a sentimental conversation about entering into a contract for their mutual support. Marriage is glamorized. Marriage is about relationships and, for some, about religiously-based commitments and vows. But marriage has also been about money: today, marriage is about the money to be made on selling weddings, and, four hundred years ago, marriage was about the value of the wife to the husband as a worker or about the value of her dowry.

Bride's Magazine conducted a survey and discovered that a typical wedding costs $19,000.[7] In some parts of the country, such as New York, average costs are closer to $31,000. In the West, $17,000 is the average.[8] These are large amounts of money for a ceremony to mark one's entry into a civil contract!

Marriage had not become a sacrament of the churches until the 12th century. Vows spoken in private before that time were sufficient to create a binding marriage, and formal marriage was typically a private contract entered into by landed families to maintain or expand their lands and wealth. In these upper classes, families essentially married other families and, in doing so, forged political and social alliances. Because these carefully negotiated contracts could be easily destroyed by a young

---

[7] http://www.weddinggazette.com/content/002165.shtml. According to the online site The Knot, the average cost may be closer to $22,000. http://www.theknot.com/ch_qaarticle.html?Object= AI980914200822 (Retrieved November 22, 2004.)

[8] One study projects $16.8 *billion* would be spent by gay couples if marriage was approved for same-sex couples. "Same-Sex Weddings The Gay-Marriage Windfall: $16.8 Billion," The Williams Project, UCLA School of Law. Retrieved November 5, 2004 from http://www1.law.ucla.edu/~williamsproj/press /marriagewindfall.html

aristocrat's whispered promises to someone else, the requirement of a public ceremony with witnesses evolved. However, at about the same time, the Protestants began turning over enforcement of these new rules to the emerging secular states.

In the 1200s, the Catholic Church formally made marriage a sacrament under canon law. Sometime in the 1500s. the Church began to require the presence of a priest and two witnesses at any marriage in an effort to better confirm paternity. Catholic Church doctrine has maintained the sacramental quality of marriage as the primary focus rather than the underlying contractual obligations and has required its followers to conform to the Church's own more strict rules about divorce or risk the loss of access to other sacraments such as communion. During the period of the 5th to the 14th centuries, the Roman Catholic Church conducted special ceremonies to bless same-sex unions. These ceremonies were nearly identical to those that blessed heterosexual unions.[9]

The Protestant idea of a *companionate marriage* evolved during the Reformation. This concept, for the first time in Western history, considered the emotional bond between a husband and a wife as an end in itself. However, it was not until the eighteenth and nineteenth centuries that romantic love became a reason for marriage. In fact, during the seventeenth century, marriage was often seen as a cure for the illness of love, although the marriage was not often to the beloved. The idea of a wife as property persisted, nonetheless. Because the wife belonged to the husband, from the 1690s to the 1870s, *wife sale* had been common in rural and small-town England. To divorce his wife, the husband would put a rope around her neck and would present her in a public sale to another man.

---

[9] For more information on same-sex unions historically, see John Boswell, *Same-Sex Unions in Premodern Europe,* (New York: Villard Books, 1994) and E.J. Graff, *What Is Marriage For? The Strange Social History of our Most Intimate Institution* (Boston, Beacon Press, 1999).

Because of the Protestant traditions brought to this country in the 1600s, marriage in America was traditionally a legal contract to be controlled by the state. Informal arrangements persisted as people scattered across a sparsely populated country without justices of the peace or ministers available to conduct ceremonies. Until recent years, children born outside of marriage were considered *bastards.* For the practical reason of not wanting to declare so many children bastards, common law marriages were recognized in most state courts if the couple consented to the relationship, cohabited and represented to others that they were married. Common law marriages still exist, though not in California.[10]

Marriage in the United States has been primarily a civil matter. A couple might elect to have a religious functionary solemnize their marriage, but the authority to legalize the marriage came from the civil government and from the license it granted the couple to marry. Nonetheless, the rights that accompany that license have often reflected other beliefs or values, most typically ones that reflect the economic and social character of the times. Women and children had long been treated as chattel, that is, as the property of the husband. A woman could not own property, enter into contracts or keep the wages she earned. New York was the first state to allow a married woman to own property, but that was not until 1848. In 1873, the U.S. Supreme Court ruled that states could prohibit women from practicing law. As late as the 1940s, twelve states still prohibited wives from entering into legal contracts.

---

[10] Alabama, Colorado, the District of Columbia, Iowa, Kansas, Montana, Rhode Island, South Carolina, Texas and Utah still allow common law marriages, each with slightly different requirements. Georgia, Idaho, Ohio, Oklahoma and Pennsylvania all had common law and still recognize relationships existing before specified dates, but they no longer recognize relationships formed after those dates. New Hampshire recognizes common law relationships for purposes of inheritance only. Only 16 of the states without common law marriage recognize common law relationships from other states. Common law relationships have been allowed only between opposite-sex couples.

Throughout most of the 1800s, the minimum age of consent for sexual intercourse in most states was 10. In Delaware, it was only seven years old. As late as the 1930s, a dozen states allowed boys as young as 14 years old to marry and permitted girls as young as 12 to marry with parental consent. Presently, 18 years old is the typical age of consent for marriages in the United States except with parental permission. Two minors – children – legally become a *man* and a *woman* by virtue of getting married. In the United States, we have allowed children to marry but not two adults of the same gender.

Under the concept of *coverture*, a woman's body also belonged to her husband. Coverture referred to a woman's status after marriage; a single woman, or *feme sole*, became known upon her marriage as a *feme covert*. Legally, after marriage, husbands and wives were treated as one entity, and the wife lost her ability to own property, enter contracts or otherwise control that which was hers. Sir William Blackstone wrote in his 1765 book, *Commentaries on the Laws of England*: "By marriage, the husband and wife are one person in law: that is, the very being or legal existence of the woman is suspended during the marriage, or at least incorporated and consolidated into that of the husband: under whose wing, protection, and *cover,* she performs every thing...." Mississippi was the first state, in 1838, to give women some rights during marriage. Laws passed in New York in 1848 began a more specific effort to eliminate the effects of coverture. One of the last vestiges of the concept was not abolished until 1975 when several state and federal laws were enacted to allow equal credit opportunity. In 1978, New York became the first state to outlaw rape in marriage. By 1990, only ten states outlawed rape in marriage; now it is a crime in every state.

Interracial marriages originally were not prohibited in this country until 1664 when Maryland became the first state to ban such marriages. This restriction continued in all states until California first eliminated the ban in 1948 in the case of *Perez* v. *Sharp*. In that case, the California Supreme Court stated: "A member of any of these races may find himself barred from marrying the person of his choice and that person to him may be irreplaceable. Human beings are bereft of worth and dignity by a doctrine that would make them as interchangeable as trains."[11] It was not until 1967 that the U.S. Supreme Court held that laws prohibiting the marriage of two people of different races were unconstitutional throughout the country.[12]

In 1987, the Rehnquist Supreme Court deemed the freedom to marry so fundamental that it could not be denied to prison inmates, even though other rights, such as voting, are routinely denied to convicted felons. Writing for the majority, Justice Sandra Day O'Connor discussed the characteristics of marriage that make it a fundamental right: 1) marriages are expressions of emotional support and public commitment, 2) the commitment of marriage may be the exercise of religious faith as well as an expression of personal dedication, 3) many inmates will be released and therefore expect the marriage to be fully consummated and 4) marital status often is a precondition to the receipt of government benefits, property rights, and other, less tangible benefits, such as the legitimation of children born out of wedlock. The Court concluded: "These incidents of marriage, like the religious and personal aspects of the marriage commitment, are unaffected by the fact of confinement...."[13]

Some other laws and court decisions show the changes in the marital relationship that many of us may have taken for granted:

- The U.S. Supreme Court in 1965 overturned laws prohibiting married couples from using contraception.

---

[11] *Perez v. Sharp,* 32 Cal. 2d 711, 726.

[12] *Loving v. Virginia*, 388 U.S. 1 (1967). Chief Justice Earl Warren, writing the majority opinion, said, "... freedom to marry or not marry a person of another race resides in that individual." It is worth noting that the Chief Justice used the word "person" rather than speaking of a man and a woman.

[13] *Turner v. Safley,* 482 U.S. 78 (1987).

- In 1971, the U.S. Supreme Court upheld an Alabama law that automatically changed a woman's legal surname to that of her husband upon marriage.
- A 1972 U.S. Supreme Court decision overturned laws prohibiting unmarried couples from purchasing contraception.
- In 1975, married women were permitted to have credit in their own name.
- In 1976, the U.S. Supreme Court overturned laws prohibiting abortions for married women without the consent of the husband.

This brief overview of the concept of marriage demonstrates that marriage is an ever changing, ever evolving social construct that will probably continue to change throughout our lifetimes.

Marriage as a Contract

If one looks at the concept of marriage from a purely legal standpoint, many of the reasons for making a distinction between marriage and civil unions seem to disappear. California currently defines marriage this way:

> Marriage is a personal relation arising out of a civil contract between a man and a woman, to which the consent of the parties capable of making that contract is necessary. Consent alone does not constitute marriage. Consent must be followed by the issuance of a license and solemnization as authorized by this division, except as provided by Section 425 and Part 4 (commencing with Section 500).[14]

Family Code section 402 makes clear that religious solemnization of the marriage is not required to make that marriage valid:

---

[14] California Family Code section 300.

> (a) No particular form for the ceremony of marriage is required for solemnization of the marriage, but the parties shall declare, in the presence of the person solemnizing the marriage and necessary witnesses, that they take each other as husband and wife.
> (b) No contract of marriage, if otherwise duly made, shall be invalidated for want of conformity to the requirements of any religious sect.

Once the couple has entered into this civil contract, the mutual obligations of a marriage contract are spelled out simply in Family Code section 720: "Husband and wife contract toward each other obligations of mutual respect, fidelity, and support." That's it. That is what marriage is: a civil contract entered into by two people,[15] obligating them to mutual respect, fidelity and support. There is nothing about procreation or children. There is nothing about religion. Marriage is a contract.

Confusion arises when religious beliefs create expectations about how the married man and woman are supposed to act and how the marriage relationship fits into the furtherance of the couple's faith and religious beliefs. It appears that most people think gays should have the same legal rights as married couples, but the institution of marriage is so imbued with religious meaning that many people's values cannot reconcile marriage and homosexuality. There are other attitudes against gay marriage which usually take a position that homosexuality is not natural. The suggestion that sexual behavior of certain types is not natural may itself have a relationship to the thinking of Thomas Aquinas and Aristotle rather that a relationship to the natural sciences of today.

It has often seemed that the gay community, in an effort to make the whole gay and lesbian issue more tolerable for the general public, hurt itself by using gentle terms such as *sexual preference* rather than *sexual orientation*. While the first term has a softer quality, the word *preference* suggested that a choice

---

[15] Still a male and a female in California as of this writing.

was possible about the gender of one's sexual partner, and the heterosexual community largely said, "Choose again!" The other difficulty has been that no matter what terminology is used, the words themselves refer to sex: sexual preference, sexual orientation, sexual partner. Although we sell things with sex in this culture, we generally do not talk openly and directly about sexual matters. Thus, the heterosexual community may also be asked to confront the issue of sex and sexual partners. Until there can be some greater understanding of the emotional and affectional aspects of same-sex relationships, more tolerance and greater willingness to confer the benefits of marriage may be slow in coming. For most of us, whether heterosexual or homosexual, the focus of life is not about sex. In most neighborhoods, we worry that Monday night the garbage cans need to be out, and the elm trees seem to be diseased and are dripping on our cars. We try to decide pressing issues such as what we are going to do with the gazillion tomatoes we all grew in our gardens this summer and whether we need to ask the city to install another traffic sign to slow cars on the cross street. We think about kids and money, are they both safe and secure? Will our parents need nursing care? Is there really a hole in the ozone?

Until the arguments in this country about marriage rights for gays can be separated from, one might say divorced from, the religious connotations attributed to marriage, there will probably need to be two types of civil contracts for relationships: marriage and civil unions or domestic partnerships. As a country, we legally abolished separate-but-equal when it comes to racial distinctions.[16] To date, including the comprehensive new California domestic partnership laws, the laws are separate but still not at all equal. The American Psychological Association, which has long recognized that gays and lesbians are entitled to equality, has issued a position paper recommending that marriage, not just domestic partnerships, be available to gay

[16] *Brown* v. *Board of Education*, 347 U.S. 483 (1954).

couples.[17] The APA is concerned not only with the larger equality issues of all people having access to marriage, but, more specifically, that discrimination and prejudice based on sexual orientation detrimentally affects a person psychologically, physically, socially, and economically. The APA also recognizes that there is a certain social status that accompanies marriage, along with various legal benefits, rights and privileges. Time will tell how these issues are resolved at the state and federal levels.

---

[17] See the complete text in Appendix C of the American Psychological Association's Resolution on Sexual Orientation and Marriage and Resolution on Sexual Orientation, Parents and Children, July 28, 2004, supporting gay *marriage*, not just civil unions.

Chapter 2

The Evolution of Domestic Partnerships in California

The first domestic partnership law was enacted in California in 1999 and became effective on January 1, 2000.[1] The law provided few rights, but it was a first step. Assembly Bill 26, authored by Carole Migden,[2] created a domestic partner registry through the Secretary of State's office, allowed registered domestic partners to see the other when one was hospitalized and required California governments to provide domestic partner benefits if that governmental unit's collective bargaining agreement allowed such benefits. Domestic partners had to be either same-sex couples or heterosexual couples, both of whom were age 62 or older, not legally married to another person and residing together. The inclusion of heterosexual couples was enacted to give some protection to older Californians who wished to join their lives but could not risk losing Social Security or other

---

[1] Most laws in California go into effect on January 1 of the year following their passage. Exceptions occur when there is great urgency for the immediate passage of a law, in which case it may become effective when signed by the governor. Or, as was true with the most recent law to expand domestic partnership rights, the law's effective date can be postponed. AB 205, passed in 2003, was specifically drafted to go into effect in 2005 rather than 2004.

[2] Such a bill would be referred to as "AB 26 (Migden)" showing that the bill originated in the Assembly with Assembly Member Migden as the primary author. We will use that form of abbreviation in referring to other legislation. A reference to legislation starting with "SB" means that the legislation originated in the Senate and is followed by the name of the senator who was the primary author.

pension or retirement benefits by marrying.

In 2001, Assembly Member Carole Migden authored another piece of legislation, AB 25, that added substantial new rights to domestic partnerships, effective January 1, 2002.

- *Right to use the stepparent adoption procedures.*[3] Stepparents are allowed to adopt their spouses' children when certain conditions are met. Previously, a gay parent could only do a second parent adoption if he or she lived in a County in which the judges were amenable to such adoptions.
- *Right to sue for wrongful death or infliction of emotional distress if a partner is killed or injured.*[4] Typically the right to sue for wrongful death exists only when there is a close blood or marriage relationship. For example, a parent could sue for the wrongful death of a child. A child could sue for the wrongful death of a parent. A spouse could sue for the wrongful death of the other spouse. Intentional infliction of emotional distress is the legal cause of action that allows damages for witnessing a situation in which your spouse, child or parent is seriously harmed or killed.
- *Right to make medical decisions for a partner.*[5] These are decisions about any care, treatment, service, or procedure, the selection of care providers and facilities, authorizations of procedures, tests and treatments and the ability to withhold water, nutrition and resuscitation, that is, "no code" decisions.
- *Right to file for state disability benefits on behalf of a disabled partner.*[6] Because a domestic partner was a legal nobody, he or she was not allowed to act on behalf of a

---

[3] California Family Code section 9000(b).

[4] California Code of Civil Procedure section 377.60; California Civil Code section 1714.01.

[5] California Probate Code section 4716.

[6] California Unemployment Insurance Code section 2705.1.

disabled partner. Now partners can file for disability benefits if their partner is unable to do so.

• *Right to be appointed conservator and to make legal and financial decisions for an incapacitated partner.*[7] By law, there is a legal presumption about who will be appointed someone's conservator if that person is not competent to make decisions for himself. The right to be conservator goes first to a spouse, then to adult children, then to parents, then to siblings and on to more distant relatives. This law places the domestic partner in the same first position of a spouse.

• *Right to use sick leave to attend to an illness of a partner or a partner's child.*[8] California allows a spouse to use sick leave for the care of his spouse or their child. This makes the same rules applicable for domestic partners.[9]

• *Right to use statutory form Wills.*[10] By law (statute), there are prescribed preprinted Wills that Californians can use. The form worked for married spouses, but previously it contained no provisions for domestic partners. The form has now been revised.

• *Right to be appointed as administrator of a partner's estate.*[11] Just as there is a legal presumption about who can be appointed conservator, the same presumption is true when someone dies without a Will: first, the spouse is appointed, then an adult child, then a parent and so forth. Administrators are appointed when there is no Will. Executors are appointed by provisions in the Will itself. The roles are essentially the same.

---

[7] California Probate Code section 1800 et seq.

[8] California Labor Code section 233.

[9] See Chapter 7 on employment-related issues for a more complete discussion.

[10] California Probate Code section 6240.

[11] California Probate Code section 8461.

• *Right to unemployment insurance benefits if you have to relocate for a partner's job.*[12] When one's spouse is required by his or her employment to relocate, the other spouse is entitled to unemployment benefits because she or he is not considered to have voluntarily quit work. This now applies to domestic partners as well.[13]

• *Requires that insurance companies offer equal health insurance coverage for domestic partners.*[14] This is binding only for insurance policies written in California. Any benefits that a spouse could receive are now available to a domestic partner.

• *Right to continued health insurance for domestic partners of deceased state employees and retirees.*[15] CalPERS and CalSTRS now must allow domestic partners to continue to receive health coverage when the domestic partner dies.

• *Right to death benefits and survivor allowances in certain counties.*[16] Los Angeles, Marin, San Mateo and Santa Barbara Counties were authorized to extend death benefits and survivor allowances to domestic partners.

• *A provision that the value of domestic partner benefits will not be taxed as income by the state.*[17] When employees were allowed to add their domestic partners to their health coverage, the IRS issued an opinion that the value of the benefits should be taxed as ordinary income to the employee. Thus, while the benefits did not cost the employee, his or her gross income and the amount of

---

[12] California Unemployment Insurance Code section 1030(a)(4).

[13] California Unemployment Insurance Code sections 1032 and 1256.

[14] California Health and Safety Code section 1374.58.

[15] California Government Code section 22871.2.

[16] California Government Code section 31780.2.

[17] California Revenue and Taxation Code section 17021.7.

withholding were increased as though the employee had been paid the value of those benefits each month.

In 2002, there was a spate of legislation that made more changes, some very specific and technical, and one that allowed a surviving domestic partner to inherit a specified share of his or her partner's estate if the partner died without a Will.[18] AB 205 (Goldberg),[19] passed in 2003, is the law which becomes effective January 1, 2005, and conveys all of the state-level rights of marriage to same-sex couples in California who are registered as domestic partners. Although this law affects rights in California, according to the Government Accountability Office (GAO), 1,138 federal laws exist in which benefits, rights and privileges are contingent on marital status or are laws in which marital status is a factor.[20] By contrast, when the GAO first researched this issue in 1997, there were 1,049 such laws.[21] These federal laws that remain unavailable to gay couples because they cannot marry are significant because they involve Social Security and Medicare benefits, federal civilian and military benefits, retirement and pension rights, death benefits, veterans' benefits, income tax and estate tax laws, immigration and naturalization issues, employment benefits, some crimes and certain family violence issues. AB 205 does everything possible to give gay couples marriage-like rights in California. However, until gays can marry and come under the provisions of these 1,138 federal laws, the rights of same-sex couples in California will approximate but not be equal to those of married heterosexual couples in the state. Additionally, most states do not have laws that make clear what

---

[18] AB 2216 (Keeley), effective July 1, 2003.

[19] See the full text of AB 205 in Appendix A.

[20] Defense of Marriage Act: Update to Prior Report, GAO-04-353R (Washington, D.C.: January 23, 2004). Available at http://www.gao.gov/new.items/d04353r.pdf.

[21] U.S. General Accounting Office, Defense of Marriage Act, GAO/OGC-97-16 (Washington, D.C.:January 31, 1997).

rights exist within that state for gay couples who were married in other states or in other countries in the world.

At the end of 2004, the Commonwealth of Massachusetts was the only state in the United States to allow same-sex marriages under laws that became effective May 17, 2004. On April 1, 2001, the Netherlands became the first country in the world to offer full marriage rights to same-sex couples. Belgium was the second country to allow full marriage rights. The law became effective January 30, 2003, but it is limited to Belgian citizens and does not allow for the adoption of children. Ontario, Canada, became the third government and the first Canadian territory to offer same-sex marriage, effective June 10, 2003. British Columbia followed suit on July 8, 2003, followed by Quebec on March 18, 2004, and the Yukon Territory on July 14, 2004. On December 9, 2004, the Canadian Supreme Court ruled that same-sex marriage was legal throughout Canada, paving the way for Canada to be the third country to fully recognize gay marriage once its Parliament passes the necessary laws.

Domestic Partners in California

As of August 2004, 25,861 couples had registered, and 1957 terminations had been filed. Because the Declaration of Domestic Partnership does not require the parties to specify their gender, the Secretary of State cannot calculate how many registrants are same-sex couples and how many are opposite-sex couples. The registrations represent more than 1600 locations. Since people from outside of California can register, some of the registrations come from other states as well as from abroad: one is from the United Kingdom and one is from Germany. Within the state, the registrations come predominantly from larger cities: Alameda has 154 couples; Bakersfield has 147; about 400 couples reside in Berkeley; Long Beach has 730 couples; Los Angeles has approximately 1725; there are over 1000 in Oakland; Sacramento has 1260; San Diego has more than 1600; and San Francisco has in excess of 3300 registered couples.

Chapter 3

The Social and Personal Implications of Domestic Partnership for Gay Couples

It is impossible to consider the new domestic partner rights and responsibilities from a solely legal perspective. In fact, those professionals, such as judges, attorneys, accountants and financial planners, who now may be involved because of these new laws, should also be aware of the larger implications of these changes. Thousands of people who never had the option to be married are suddenly going to have the closest[1] thing to marriage in California: a domestic partnership.[2] With the exception of state income taxes, in every law in California where there is now a reference to a spouse, one must interpret that law to apply to domestic partners. Where the law refers to being married, the law applies in exactly the same way if a person is a registered domestic partner. If the law refers to a "husband" or "wife," it must be read to apply to a registered domestic partner.

Isn't this what gay couples have wanted for so long? In fact, it is what many gay couples have wanted, but it is easy to anticipate some period of adjustment as gay couples learn the practical aspects of domestic partnership and learn to operate in

---

[1] If you believe in Freudian slips, you might find it interesting that the word "closest" in this sentence was misspelled "closet" in the first draft of this chapter. Maybe domestic partnerships *are* the closet version of marriage.

[2] This chapter focuses solely on gay couples, since heterosexual couples who take advantage of these laws have the legal right to marry, often have been married previously and do not face the same discrimination.

this new system to which they have never had access.

Strangers in a Strange Land

Consider the analogy of immigrants from a country with a native language other than English. When these people reach the United States, they can often be overwhelmed by the new customs, the new rules, the foreign quality of everything around them. They may have read and heard about the United States, they may have friends and family already living in the United States, and they may have always wanted to immigrate here, and, suddenly, here they are. Transfer this image to this new Country of Marriage. Granted, the immigrants are not going to be able to go directly to Marriage, but they will get to the nearest country, Domestic Partnership. It will have to do for now, but it will be tolerable because the two destinations are nearly identical.

For these newcomers, there may be some disappointment that they were not allowed to enter the Country of Marriage, but even this new land of Domestic Partnership is unfamiliar. There are suddenly rules about owning property with one's life partner. Just the day before, there were none. Now, there may be responsibilities for your own debts *and* those of your life partner. Just the day before, you were each on your own. The property you have each purchased during your partnership now may belong to both of you. Just the day before, it was yours alone. If your relationship fails and you want to separate, you must go through various procedures, some of which may require you to go to court and will cost you money. Just the day before, you simply could have walked away. What's more, all of these terms and requirements seem so technical, and they are in a foreign language! Just the day before, you did not even have to think about these things.

Think of another analogy: one day you suddenly have the opportunity to start a business of your own. You have wanted to do this for years, but now, it is actually going to happen. You need a place to conduct your business. You need equipment and stock and employees. You have to negotiate the world of leases and contracts and payroll and withholding taxes and workers' compensation insurance that you never have dealt with before. You need a business license and perhaps other permits. There's insurance. Maybe you have decided to incorporate for various reasons, and now you have to deal with corporate filings and minutes and fees. Your head is spinning! You've been around businesses before, and you've heard your family and friends talk about some of these things, but you never had to understand them all before because they never applied to you! Perhaps a more humorous example is to imagine a dog chasing a car. Have you ever wondered what the dog would do if he caught the car? The dog might wonder too: now that I have it, what do I do?

None of this is meant to suggest that gay couples do not want the option of domestic partnerships. Rather, this is what January 1, 2005 may have felt like for many gay couples. For the gay couples and those who assist them in this new land, there is going to be a period both of confusion and of education. People may not know what they can do and what they cannot do. Professionals and the heterosexual majority may not even think in the broader terms of how this all applies and how it might confound gay couples. One minor example: one can transfer ownership of a car between spouses or between parent and child without paying sales tax to the Department of Motor Vehicles when registering the car. Will the gay domestic partner and the clerk at DMV know or think that this exception applies to this transfer of title?

Coming Out as Domestic Partners

There is another component that perhaps is even more basic to this shift in the law: to claim these rights, people will have to declare to others – to the clerk at DMV, to the loan officer, to their physician – that they are domestic partners. This means gay individuals will have to *come out*.

Coming out is a lifelong process of deciding when and if,

and then, how, to reveal to others that one is gay. Heterosexuals do not need to come out because there is a presumption that people are heterosexual, and one can reveal the gender of a spouse often just by revealing the person's name or by using words such as *husband* or *wife*. Many heterosexuals make public their marital status by having pictures of their spouses and kids at work. For a gay person, disclosure of the existence of a domestic partner may require something specific to be said. Most gays have differing levels of comfort about being out depending upon the setting. For example, a gay person may be open with friends and perhaps with family, but they might be less open at work or with a landlord where they believe negative reactions could have far greater negative repercussions.

Dozens of books have been written about the coming out process. It is hard for many non-gays to understand. This is a society in which many people still believe homosexuality is immoral or wrong or the result of mental illness. Because gays grow up in the dominant culture, many have internalized some of these same beliefs. Many gay people have been the victims of discrimination and hate crimes. Many have chosen to be very selective in whom they tell about being gay. For some, their families are convinced that the person with whom they live is "just a roommate."

Perhaps, though, these same gay couples have taken the legal steps to become domestic partners. Now, to claim their rights, they must go public; they have to come out as domestic partners! This may take some adjustment for everyone. Becoming a domestic partner is not going to change certain other people's views of homosexuality. In much the same way that a parent with a bias against interracial marriages will not magically become tolerant because his child has now married someone of a different race, a family will not suddenly change its views about homosexuality because their child has become a domestic partner with someone of the same gender. In fact, the feelings may become more entrenched with the impending permanency and with the potentially more public nature of these relationships.

Individuals are going to have to say to the loan officer who is helping with a home loan or to the benefits officer at work or to the DMV clerk, "I have a domestic partner." Perhaps, for some gay couples, this will be easy. For many, it will be hard or at least bring a moment of pause as they assess the situation. Years ago, a client came to my office to probate her father's estate. Within the next four months, her grandmother and her mother also died. We dealt with the business of the estates and the peculiarities of having three probates going simultaneously. She lived under a blanket of grief. At one point I suggested that it would be good for her to have a Will for herself so similar confusion could be avoided for her beneficiaries. She said, "I'm not sure you'll want to do a Will for me." I was startled and asked why she would think that. She answered, "Because I'm gay." During all those months we had spent working together, she had kept her personal life a secret from me, and still she was worried that I would not want to help her with her basic legal rights. In addition, she assumed a serious lapse in my compassion because she was not heterosexual.

The people who serve these gay couples are not going to be without their own biases. For example, a survey in California showed that law firms were less inclined to hire attorneys who were gay or lesbian despite ethical mandates to avoid discrimination against others on the basis of sexual orientation. In the article, "Gay, Lesbian Lawyers Win Bar Support" in the October 1996 issue of the *California Bar Journal*, the State Bar reported on a random sample survey of 14,300 members to determine if there were significant differences between gay, lesbian, bisexual and other members of the bar. The study found numerous disturbing results: 1) after 10 years in the profession, 26% of the gay lawyers were partners in law firms, as opposed to 38% of the non-gay lawyers; 2) of those lawyers in practice for fewer than 10 years, 4% of the gay lawyers were partners, compared to 11% of the non-gay attorneys; 3) after 10 years of practice, 41% of non-gay lawyers earned more than $125,000, yet just 27% of gay attorneys had a similar income; 4) 12% said their office partners or supervisors preferred not to work with gay attorneys; 5) more than 8% of the attorneys said that their offices denied gay attorneys work simply because they were gay; 6) more than 11% saw or experienced sexual orientation bias in attorney work assignments. The State Bar also reported that openly gay attorney job applicants and even heterosexual applicants who supported gay causes had a difficult time getting interviews. As an example, the report tells of an instance involving a heterosexual applicant who spent a summer working at National Gay Rights Advocates. He did not get a single job interview until he removed the reference from his resume. Within the legal profession itself, in a 2001 survey, only 1.3% of the members identified as gay and .8% as lesbian.[3] Either there is a disproportionately low number of gays and lesbians in the field of law or they are afraid to come out within their own profession. Either way, will these legal professionals be available and open to serving the needs of domestic partners?

Will the court system deal well with these gay couples? Courts can be slow to change. Though ethically obligated to avoid discrimination against people because of their sexual orientation,[4] judges are human beings who are products of this society. Biases will exist. Those biases may be subtle, as in displaying a tendency toward *heterosexism*, that is, a belief that being heterosexual is preferable or desirable. Heterosexism might lead a court to give less credence to a request for spousal support because these are two adults with no children, both of the same gender and both therefore more equal in their prospective earning abilities. If this were a man and a woman divorcing, would the court make the same order? A court could see the request for a domestic violence restraining order as less serious

---

[3] *Final Report: California Bar Journal Survey, September 10, 2001*, p. 3.

[4] Cal Rules of Court, Appx, Canon 3B(5).

because these are two people of the same gender, so the fight is characterized as a mutual fight rather than a serious and dangerous situation between two people who see themselves as the spouses of the other. If this were a man and a woman fighting, would the court make the same order? For some gay couples, even the act of going to court involves having to come out in a public setting. Sensitivity by the courts will be necessary.

One example points out how simplistically situations can be viewed when they involve two people of the same sex, to the detriment of the parties. I litigated a case in another state on behalf of a woman who had become romantically involved with her female pastor. The pastor had induced the woman to contribute many thousands of dollars toward buying a rental property together with the promise that someday they would live in one of the units together. The pastor was still in a civil union with another woman, but told my client that the relationship had ended. When time came to take title, the pastor put it in her name alone, but did not reveal this to my client who continued to contribute to maintenance and upkeep for the property. The pastor later ended the relationship and started living with yet another woman. When the pastor put the property up for sale, my client was alerted to the title problem and brought suit after informal resolution efforts were rebuffed. The judge made many inconsistent rulings. He tried to characterize my client and the pastor as married and, in doing so, minimized the reality that the pastor had used her position to seduce my client into a relationship. At the same time, he then concluded that same-sex couples had no marital rights under that state's laws, and so he treated them as legal strangers. Had the pastor been married and a man, her misconduct and abuse of her position of trust easily would likely have been seen as unethical and exploitive.

What are the implications of these social realties for many gay couples? Some will not avail themselves of domestic partnerships. Some will tread cautiously into this new land of domestic partnerships. Some will walk openly into this new land

and claim their rights. For both the gay person and the professional, there will undoubtedly be a learning process because such a large group of disenfranchised people now have the legitimacy and strength of the law behind them.

We will undoubtedly be challenged as the domestic partnership laws go into effect: challenged as gay people, as professionals, as a state. We will each need to look at our biases and assumptions, and we will need to think creatively as we determine how domestic partnerships will function in practice. We need to be careful in assuming that everything is just the same for gays as for heterosexuals, other than the gender of their partners. Gays have been discriminated against and marginalized. It is important to contemplate the implications of that experience as these new rights and responsibilities are exercised.

Chapter 4

AB 205 in a Nutshell[1]

So what makes AB 205 so important? What does it really say? The heart of the matter is in Family Code section 297.5(a) that reads:

> Registered domestic partners shall have the same rights, protections, and benefits, and shall be subject to the same responsibilities, obligations, and duties under law, whether they derive from statutes, administrative regulations, court rules, government policies, common law, or any other provisions or sources of law, *as are granted to and imposed upon spouses.* [emphasis added]

In the most basic terms, this means that, other than laws relating to state income taxes, any California law that now refers to *spouses* or *marriage* or uses the terms *husband* or *wife* must be interpreted to read *domestic partner* as well.

The implications of these changes in the law may often be subtle. The law that requires a judge to disqualify himself or herself from a case because the judge is personally aware of disputed evidence in the case is a good example. The law presumes that a judge does have such personal knowledge of the evidence if the judge or the judge's spouse, children and grandchildren, or the parents, siblings and nieces and nephews

---

[1] For you non-lawyers reading this, the "nutshell" books were a series of short books that condensed the whole subject matter of an area of law for study and cramming, much like Cliff Notes for literature.

and their spouses of either the judge or the judge's spouse may be a material witness in the case.[2] What does this mean in real life?

> It's Thanksgiving Day. Judge Marshall and his wife are at her parents' house for dinner. This year, his wife's nephew Phillip arrives with a friend named Gene. No one says anything, and the two men are very discreet, but it is understood among the family members that Gene is Phillip's significant other. Dinner is served, everyone eats, watches a football game afterwards, and chats a bit as they keep going back for leftovers. The judge meets Gene, and they talk about mundane things. Six weeks later in a lawsuit before the judge, the defendant calls his employee, Gene, as a material witness. The judge takes a few minutes to figure out how he knows Gene and remembers the Thanksgiving dinner.
>
> Under AB 205, the judge should treat Gene as the spouse of Phillip and disqualify himself from hearing the case. However, although the judge assumed Phillip and Gene were same-sex partners, he does not know for sure. Even if they are in a relationship, the judge does not know if they are registered domestic partners to whom AB 205 applies.
>
> What happens if the judge raises the issue openly in the courtroom in front of Gene's employer? Might this *outing* cost Gene his job? Might jurors view Gene's testimony differently if they think he's gay? The judge's obligation to disqualify himself in such a situation is mandatory. What should he do?

The law in this case requires the judge to recuse himself. If the judge does not disqualify himself when he knows he should, the case could later be appealed or reversed. An appeal or new

---

[2] California Code of Civil Procedure section 170.1 says, in part:
(a) A judge shall be disqualified if any one or more of the following is true: (1) The judge has personal knowledge of disputed evidentiary facts concerning the proceeding. A judge shall be deemed to have personal knowledge within the meaning of this paragraph if the judge, or the *spouse of the judge*, or a person within the third degree of relationship to either of them, or the *spouse of such a person* is to the judge's knowledge likely to be a material witness in the proceeding. [emphasis added]

trial would cost the parties a great deal of money that they may not have. If a judge disobeys the law, he may be subject to discipline by the Judicial Council. There are ways the judge can resolve the matter, but if Gene is not *out* with his employer, his employer may learn that Gene is gay or certainly wonder what the connection is that has caused the commotion.

Annually, when a physician renews his or her medical license, the physician must declare whether he or any immediate family member owns an interest in a health-related facility, such as a laboratory, physical therapy office or diagnostic imaging facility.[3] The definition of "immediate family" includes the spouse of a child of the physician.[4] The point of the law is to disclose financial interests that physicians have in other health facilities from which they might benefit by referring patients to those facilities.

> Dr. Wilson is a family practice physician. He has three adult children, one of whom he believes is a lesbian. They have never talked about the issue directly, but he knows that his daughter has lived with the same woman for the last six years. He and his daughter have informally agreed not to discuss the issue of the nature of her relationship with her *roommate*. The roommate owns a physical therapy practice. What must the physician do when he renews his medical license?

The law in this case obligates the doctor to report the ownership of the physical therapy practice because it is owned by the spouse of his child, presuming they are registered domestic partners. Does he report it or convince himself that he does not have enough information to be required to make a report?

There are other important aspects of AB 205. "Former registered domestic partners" shall have all the rights and

---

[3] California Business and Professions Code section 2426(a).

[4] California Business and Professions Code section 2426(b)(4).

responsibilities of former spouses. This means, in effect, that divorce laws apply to the end of a domestic partnership and that there will be issues of spousal support and division of property. The law also says that a surviving registered domestic partner shall have all the rights of a surviving spouse. This would include the right to inherit the deceased partner's estate when there is no Will and the right to serve as administrator of the deceased partner's estate.

The rights and responsibilities of the two domestic partners will be the same as the rights of spouses when it comes to children of the relationship. If the partners have a child during their domestic partnership, the child shall be presumed to be theirs jointly, and, on dissolution of the relationship, there will be custody and child support issues.

The only exception about equality in state law relates to income taxes:

> Notwithstanding this section, in filing their state income tax returns, domestic partners shall use the same filing status as is used on their federal income tax returns, or that would have been used had they filed federal income tax returns. Earned income may not be treated as community property for state income tax purposes. [Family Code section 297.5(g)]

In practical terms, this means that there will not be an option for treating a registered domestic partner as a spouse for purposes of claiming dependents or in determining what tax rate schedule one must use. The prohibition on treating earned income as community property means each partner will be on her own when it comes to tax liability.

James and Alex are registered domestic partners. James is employed with an income of $60,000 per year. Alex is completing his Master's degree and earned $15,000 last year working part-time.

The law in this case will require each partner to file separate state and federal returns as single persons, claim such deductions as are legally appropriate for single individuals and use the single rate for determining their respective taxes. They would not be able to claim each other as a dependent. If James and Alex were married, they could file joint state and federal tax returns and apply all appropriate deductions and use the tax schedule for married couples.

The income tax issue becomes slightly more complicated by the provision of the new law that says, "The rights and obligations of registered domestic partners with respect to a child of either of them shall be the same as those of spouses."[5] The question that logically follows is that if the child is to be considered a child of the relationship and if both domestic partners have an obligation to support the child, then who will claim the child as a dependent on income tax returns? As of this writing, there is no definitive answer.

Domestic partnership registrations from outside of California must be recognized on the same basis as the California domestic partnerships. The out-of-state partnerships must be a legal union of two persons of the same sex, other than a marriage, that is substantially equivalent to the California registered domestic partnerships. At this point, Vermont's civil union appears to meet these standards. New Jersey's Domestic Partner Act probably does as well. However, because the law excludes marriages, marriages in Canada or in Massachusetts[6]

[5] Family Code section 297.5(d).

[6] Massachusetts is considering legislation that would bar same-sex marriages and instead create civil unions. If this happens, California would likely recognize those unions under the domestic partner laws.

would not trigger domestic partner rights under the California law.

The remaining portions of AB 205 are essentially procedural, dealing with the process of applying the law such as identifying who qualifies to be domestic partners, explaining the registration process and defining a summary termination[7] process. The law also requires that state documents and forms be revised to be inclusive of domestic partners. The California Judicial Council, which is responsible for all the standard legal forms used in courts, has completed its process for developing new forms for domestic partners for use in petitioning for dissolution, legal separation or nullity.[8]

---

[7] The summary termination process is explained in detail in Chapter 11. This is an abbreviated process for those who meet specific criteria and allows the couple to avoid the need for a dissolution action.

[8] Partners who do not qualify for the summary termination process must go to family law court to obtain a dissolution, legal separation or a nullity. A nullity is a legal annulment. These processes are discussed in more detail in Chapter 12.

Chapter 5

The Closet and the New Law

> You may be tempted to skip this chapter to get to the heart of the law. Please do not. The issues in this chapter are the filter through which all the legal issues must be viewed.

As this book was coming together, the issue that emerged again and again was the issue of the *coming out* experience for gays and lesbians. So many of the examples in this book could easily be read and dismissed. "What's the big deal?" a reader might ask. How hard could it be for a judge to disqualify or recuse himself because his wife's nephew's domestic partner is a material witness in a case? It probably would not be hard at all for the judge, but it might be very hard for the gay person. It will be hard for others who are close to the gay person as well.

There is no easy way to describe the experience of being gay and having to come out day after day and time after time. Some choose not to come out at all. Two women have been together nineteen years and raised six children. They have not registered as domestic partners because one is afraid that anyone could go to the Secretary of State's office and find her name as a domestic partner and *out* her at work,[1] which could bring serious repercussions. She's right: the documents at the Secretary of State's office are public records, and, for a fairly minimal amount, one can buy the mailing list. Marriage licenses are public records, so domestic partner registration records should also be public.

---

[1] To *out* her means to disclose without her permission that she is gay.

It may be difficult to understand the seriousness and the pervasiveness of the coming out process. It is hard to find a good metaphor to convey the range of emotions and the risks that prevail in the gay community daily. Despite the improving conditions socially, many are still afraid. Some have been the victims of hate crimes. Dr. Gregory Herek at the University of California, Davis, has conducted one of the largest studies to date on the incidence and effects of hate crimes. In a study done in the Metropolitan Sacramento, California, area, he found that nearly one-fifth of lesbians and more than a quarter of gay men had been victims of hate crimes. Not only was the frequency important, but he found that recent hate crime victims suffered significantly more depression, anger, anxiety and post-traumatic stress than did victims of non-bias crimes. These subjects also manifested significantly more fear of crime, greater perceived vulnerability, less belief in the benevolence of people, a lower sense of mastery, and more attributions of their personal setbacks to sexual prejudice than did non-bias crime victims and non-victims.[1] Individuals often have been thrown out of their homes by their parents.[2] Others have been shunned, degraded, even damned by their religious institutions.[3] Many have lost their jobs or their housing. Matthew Shepard was beaten to death.

---

[1] Herek, G. M., Gillis, J. R. & Cogan, J.C. (1999). Psychological sequelae of hate crime victimization among lesbian, gay and bisexual adults. *Journal of Consulting and Clinical Psychology, 67*(6), 945-951.

[2] One woman, forced out of her family's home by her mother and stepfather when she was just 17, has not seen her parents in the ensuing twenty-five years. The woman is not welcome back until she abandons what they consider to be her disgraceful way of life. The woman has an advanced degree, a good career, two children she adopted and is a contributing member of her community. As far as she knows, her parents have no idea that they have grandchildren.

[3] In one instance, an orthodox Jewish temple conducted an entire death ritual for a woman member of their congregation when she admitted she was gay, and it is now as though she is dead to those members.

> The Rev. Ed Sherriff, associate pastor of the Sacramento Metropolitan Community Church, a church with a primary outreach to the gay, lesbian, bisexual and transgendered communities, told of his experience as a young man with his church. He had married and had children, thinking his attraction to men would go away if he married. At some point early in his career, his church leadership learned that he might be homosexual. During a Sunday service, he was unexpectedly called up to the podium and in front of his parishioners, his wife and his daughters, the church fathers labeled him a homosexual and banished him from the church. It was more than twenty years later before he stepped into another church, and, when he did, he said he cried and cried on that day. Rev. Ed ran a thrift store and food program outreach in one of the more needy areas of Sacramento. He was murdered in 1999, stabbed multiple times by men who broke into his home. The killer, out on parole fewer than three months, later justified his actions by claiming that the pastor had made sexual advances to the killer's nephew. The nephew testified he had never seen the pastor. Even in death, his sexual orientation was being used against him – by his murderer.

Because sexual orientation is not a racial or physical trait, a gay person's defining characteristics are invisible. As a result, most gay people can maneuver in the community and *pass* as heterosexual if they choose. A consequence of this invisibility is that many either have to endure the deceptions they create or they must make a deliberate choice to say or do something that will identify them as gay.

One of the long-standing complaints has been, "Why do gay people have to flaunt being gay?" Unless one says something in conversation or uses a behavior such as holding a partner's hand, others may not know the person is gay. Saying something may be the only way to let another person know that one is gay. Two heterosexual people holding hands in public probably would not be accused of flaunting anything.

Picture this example: two middle-aged women, partners of many years, need a new bed. They go to a nearby store to check out mattresses. There are dozens on display, and one woman lies down on a bed. The other lies down on a different bed. The first beckons to her partner to come try the mattress she is lying on. The second woman is reluctant about *coming out* to the salesman. If they both lie on the mattress together, as they will when they get it home, the salesman might think they are gay. What's wrong with that? It's that the salesman may think they are gay, and the women do not know what kind of attitude or service or help to expect as a result. Will they be treated like any other customers? Will the salesman say something unkind? Or will he hold his tongue to get the sale, but forget little things, such as telling the women of a new delivery promotion the store is offering or perhaps delay their delivery or do something else to show his disdain or dislike?

Perhaps choosing a new mattress set should not be a coming out experience, but it can be. The couple has to decide for whom they are buying the mattress, the salesperson or themselves? There are so many other ways in which it is possible to have a need to come out: opening a joint bank account, telling the auto insurance representative who this other person is who needs to be on your insurance policy so the couple can claim discounts available to married couples, explaining to the contractor who is remodeling your bathroom why he is to take direction from the other adult in the house about any decisions to be made, and trying to decide which box to check for marital status on the information form at the doctor's office and whether to write down your partner's name as the emergency contact.

The fact that you are reading this book means either you are in or are contemplating a domestic partnership or you are interested in helping domestic partners deal with the realities and legalities of the new laws. It might be easy for you to dismiss any of the previous examples as nothing to worry about, knowing that if you were the bank teller or insurance representative or contractor or doctor that you would have no problem with the person identifying as gay. In fact, you might hope they would be forthcoming. Much of the rest of the world does not, however, share the same degree of egalitarianism, empathy and understanding. It is certain that others are not always hostile, but there are many people with deeply ingrained attitudes and judgments about and against gay people. It is the consternation and the anxiety which arises again and again, in surprisingly simple situations, that are the problems for gays. Do I come out and get what I want or maybe I won't get what I want by coming out? Or do I stay in the closet and not get what I want or maybe I'll get it anyway even by staying in the closet? Maybe I don't want it after all.

There is also much religious condemnation of gays. At its worst, gays are an abomination who should face everlasting judgment. At best, they must remain celibate and not act out their immoral sexual attitudes and proclivities. They are, by turns, shunned, judged, banished, disdained, feared and hated.[4] We often attribute negative characteristics to groups against which we have discriminated in this country: lazy, dumb, slow, shiftless, shrewd, dishonest, childlike, gullible, ugly – and the list goes on. For gays, the list usually starts with terms such as "immoral," "sinful," "disturbed," "deviant," "sick," "disgusting" and terms far more pejorative. The terms are not so much about characteristics and attributes as they are about one's very being and soul, one's essence.

For whatever motivation, some people think they must condemn gays because they believe the Bible condemns gays. This book is not the forum in which to address the religious debates about the intentions of a higher power toward gays and lesbians. Nor is it a forum for clarification or discussion of the

---

[4] In the Counseling Gays and Lesbians class I have taught for many years at California State University, Sacramento, I have used a questionnaire for the students to answer anonymously. The students are all Master's degree students preparing to be counselors. This is not a scientific sampling. Anecdotally, the statements that a number of students have trouble agreeing with are: 1) homosexuals should be allowed to teach elementary school, 2) I would feel comfortable going to a doctor of my same gender who was gay, 3) homosexuals should be allowed to adopt children, and 4) homosexuals should be allowed to marry.

Bible. Since there are in excess of 270 different versions of the Bible, and because we learn more daily about the cultures and languages of Biblical times, it seems difficult to claim that *the* Bible condemns gays and that it follows that believers must do so too. Which Bible? Translated when? By whom? And who determines which prohibitions found in scripture are valid for this time?

It warrants repeating, however, that coming out is an ongoing experience, that there is rejection and condemnation and misunderstanding in every important venue of life for the gay person. Most significant for the context of this book is that exercising one's rights demands coming out for the gay individual and for the gay couple.[5]

Gays are often the subject of blatant, subtle or even unconscious judgment because of their purported immorality. Knowing, as most gay people do, that there are many in the world with such judgments, coming out is frightening and rarely done lightly or casually. Back to the mattress salesman: is the gay couple going to act in such a way, although discreetly and properly, so that the mattress salesman understands that they are buying the mattress set for their shared bed in their bedroom in their home?

One other aspect of the coming out experience requires attention for those who are going to help domestic partners navigate these new rights and responsibilities: in gay relationships, the degree of comfort each partner may have about being out is not always shared equally. One member of the couple may feel reasonably comfortable being out. His or her partner, for whatever reason, may feel less comfortable or want to be open

---

[5] In October 2004, the California Fair Political Practices Commission determined that gay and lesbian public officials with domestic partners must comply with the same financial disclosure requirements as married spouses. Public officials would be required to make public disclosures of property, considered community property with their domestic partners, and public officials could not vote or make decisions in their governmental capacity that would affect those mutual interests and create a conflict of interest.

only with close friends or family. Sometimes a person will be open with one parent but not the other or with one sibling but not others.[6] Being out is not all-or-nothing: it is developmental, temporal, situational and relational.

Understanding the fluidity of the coming out experience will help those who will provide services for domestic partners. Taking a risk to come out to those professionals who can help is necessary for those in a partnership or for those entering a domestic partnership.

---

[6] A colleague, a professional woman in her late forties, shared with me the story of recently coming out to her parents. She spent the weekend with her parents who live several hundred miles distant. Before she left to return to her home, the woman spoke to her mother who was alone in the kitchen. She told her mother that the reason she wasn't married after all these years was that she was a lesbian. Her mother absorbed the information but cautioned her daughter to not tell her father because, "He couldn't handle it." Packing her car later that day, the woman was alone with her father. She found the words to tell him, and his first comment was, "Don't tell your mother. It would break her heart."

Chapter 6

Becoming Domestic Partners

Reading AB 205

If you are the type of person who likes to go to the source, the entire text of AB 205 is included in Appendix A. Laws are hard to read for most people, largely because they seem to be written in a foreign language. It is not so much that the language is foreign as it is *formal*. The heart of AB 205 says, "Registered domestic partners *shall* have the same rights, protections, and benefits, and *shall* be subject to the same responsibilities, obligations, and duties under law, ... as are granted to and imposed upon spouses." It is important to pay attention to the distinctions in a law that says something *may* be done, which is permissive or discretionary, versus where the law says it *shall* be done, which is mandatory and obligatory. The treatment of registered domestic partners in the same manner as spouses is obligatory, according to the law's language. One also must watch when words are used such as "and," "all," "or," "if" and "except," just to name a few. Those words often set conditions.

One of the basic principles of the interpretation of laws is that you must give a law its most basic meaning: one should not torture the meaning of the words to force them into a desired outcome. If you wish to read the law itself, a few other pieces of information may help you negotiate the text. This law is typical to most laws in its format. The Assembly Bill number appears at the top followed by a chapter number. All bills that are enacted each year become chapters that are compiled in the statutes (laws) for that year. AB 205, once it was signed into law, became Chapter 421 of the Statutes of 2003, the year it was passed and signed into law. The authors and co-authors of the bill in both the Assembly and Senate are listed. The summary under the chapter number describes what specific laws are created, repealed or modified.[7] The Legislative Counsel then writes a summary of what the law does and any financial effects the law may have.

The rest of the law typically is laid out in a standard order: first, there is a portion that explains the Legislature's intent behind the law, followed by the name of the law,[8] followed by sections that define relevant terms. Next comes the substance of the law, that is, what is being enacted or legislated. In AB 205, these are the sections that define the rights of domestic partners. Once the law that is the focus of the legislation is laid out, any exceptions or limitations to the law are defined along with any other procedural components of the law. Procedural components are laws that define the processes involved in applying the main focus of the act, describe special situations or mandate certain forms.

Requirements to be Domestic Partners

There are a number of primary conditions that individuals must meet to become domestic partners. Underlying the technical requirements is the primary requirement: "Domestic partners are two adults who have chosen to share one another's lives in an intimate and committed relationship of mutual caring."[9]

Common residence. The two adults must share a common residence.[10] This does not require that they are both on

---

[7] California assembles its laws in 29 different codes. The codes are a collection of laws related to a common topic. Most of the laws involving domestic partners are in the Family Code. For your interest, all of the codes are listed in Appendix B.

[8] This is only included if there is a group of related laws enacted at once rather than if the law only adds or modifies a few sections of existing law. The collection of laws relating to one topic is typically referred to as an *Act*. In this case, the law defines itself as "The California Domestic Partner Rights and Responsibilities Act of 2003."

[9] Family Code section 297(a).

[10] Family Code section 297(b)(1).

the lease or on the deed or title to the home, only that they consider this their primary residence. The domestic partner law itself spells out more information about the question of common residence:

> "Have a common residence" means that both domestic partners share the same residence. It is not necessary that the legal right to possess the common residence be in both of their names. Two people have a common residence even if one or both have additional residences. Domestic partners do not cease to have a common residence if one leaves the common residence but intends to return.[11]

Unmarried or no partner.[12] At the time of entering into the relationship, neither person can be married to someone else nor can they be a member of another domestic partnership unless that partnership has been terminated. If a previous domestic partnership has ended due to the death of one partner, there is no requirement to formally terminate the partnership before entering into a new domestic partnership. One must also terminate or dissolve the previous domestic partnership before marrying anyone other than one's registered domestic partner.[13] The earlier domestic partnership law caused a termination of the partnership upon the marriage of one partner. This condition no longer exists.

Limitations on blood relationships. The law that controls who can be domestic partners has the same limitations as the laws relating to marriage, that is, the couple may not be related by blood. Half-siblings could not be domestic partners because there is still a common parent. Step-siblings could be domestic partners because their connection to each other is created by the marriage of their parents, and the two would not be

---

[11] Family Code section 297(c).

[12] Family Code section 297(b)(2).

[13] Family Code section 298.5(c).

related by blood.

Both partners are adults. Domestic partner must be at least 18 years of age. There is no provision for a parent to consent to a minor entering a domestic partnership. If both partners are of the same sex, there is no further age restriction. If the partners are different sexes, then at least one of the partners must be 62 years of age or older *and* one or both of the partners must meet the eligibility criteria under Title II of the Social Security Act as defined in 42 U.S.C. Section 402(a) for old-age insurance benefits or Title XVI of the Social Security Act as defined in 42 U.S.C. Section 1381 for aged individuals.[14] Some individuals would face a loss or reduction in various Social Security old age and disability benefits or other pensions and death benefits if they remarried, so this law allows opposite-sex couples to live together with many of the same protections of marriage.

Both partners are capable of consenting.[15] Consent to any binding relationship or contract is presumed possible only for adults, that is, someone 18 years of age or older. Thus, a minor is not able to borrow money, sign leases or buy a home. This requirement of consent again points out that only adults may be domestic partners. However, consent also requires that a person have sufficient mental capacity to consent. If someone were under the influence of alcohol or drugs and impaired in his or her ability to reason, the consent to the partnership could be voided. Likewise, if there were undue influence or duress involved in forcing one or both people to sign the consent, then, that, too, might negate the stated consent. It is unusual for anyone to be compelled to marry. One must obtain a license, have the relationship solemnized and return the license to the county for registration. For a domestic partnership, there is only a form to fill out, but the signatures of the parties must be notarized which

---

[14] Under the first domestic partnership law in 1999, AB 26, both parties had to be 62 or older. Now, only one partner must be at least 62 years old.

[15] Family Code section 297(a)(6).

requires an additional step. The likelihood of someone forcing another person into a domestic partnership is remote.[16]

The Registration Process

Becoming domestic partners is a simple process that requires completing a form and filing it along with a minimal fee. Considering that domestic partners will have many of the same rights as marriage, the process is amazingly simple.

Declaration of Domestic Partnership. The Secretary of State's office prepares the required forms and distributes them to each county clerk in addition to having the forms available in its offices and online.[17] The form requires that both partners confirm that they meet the requirements for being domestic partners. They must provide a mailing address. The forms require, as of January 1, 2005, that the partners consent to jurisdiction of the Superior Courts of California for the purpose of dissolving or obtaining a nullity of their partnership and for any other proceeding that relates to determining their rights and responsibilities toward each other.[18] This consent applies even if one or both of the partners ceases to be a resident of, or maintain a domicile in, California. The requirement of consent to the California courts' jurisdiction recognizes that domestic partnership is a right limited to the State of California. As a result, if one or both of the parties leave California and are no longer residents of the state, they likely would not find another court with the authority

---

[16] The rules relating to notaries state: "The completion of an acknowledgment that contains statements that the notary public knows to be false not only may cause the notary to be liable for civil penalties and administrative action, but is also a criminal offense." A notary who knows that the information on the registration form is not true may be liable if he or she notarizes the document nonetheless. California Secretary of State, 2004 Notary Public Handbook . http://www.ss.ca.gov/business/notary/notary_2004hdbk.htm#ack (Retrieved August 15, 2004).

[17] Family Code section 298. Online form: http://www.ss.ca.gov/dpregistry/forms/sf-dp1.pdf

[18] Family Code section 298(c).

to dissolve their partnership. The law therefore specifically allows them to return in order to use the California courts.[19]

The last requirement for the Declaration of Domestic Partnership is that both partners' signatures be notarized. The notary signs and stamps an *acknowledgment* that states that he or she has affirmed the identity of the person signing the document, so valid identification will be needed. Notaries typically charge a fee for their services, usually ten dollars for each signature notarized.

The completed Declaration then must be sent to or taken to the Secretary of State's office where the Secretary of State will register the Declaration in the state registry and will return a copy of the form along with a ceremonial Certificate of Domestic Partnership to the partners' mailing address.[20]

Filing a false declaration. AB 205 has created a misdemeanor crime for filing an intentionally and materially false Declaration of Domestic Partnership.[21] For example, if one or both of the individuals filing the Declaration know that either of them does not meet the qualifications, but they file nonetheless, perhaps so they can take advantage of health insurance benefits, this could be prosecuted as a misdemeanor. Misdemeanors are typically punishable by up to one year in a county jail or a fine or both. Depending on the purpose for filing the false Declaration,

---

[19] This is another of those instances in which forming a domestic partnership is a "get real" experience for the gay couples who become partners. Because marriage was not an option and because there were no rights and responsibilities accompanying the fact of a gay couple living together or making an emotional commitment to each other, the custom has been simply to part, divide things up as much as the couple can work out and then move on. Domestic partnerships, however, do not end because the two parties separate. The parties must formally dissolve their partnership, and they cannot legally enter another partnership before dissolving the existing one.

[20] Family Code section 298.5(b). Something is material when it is critical to the legal right, responsibility or process. In this situation, if one partner had not legally terminated a previous partnership, that would be a materially false statement.

[21] Family Code section 298(c).

the partners could be subject to other civil or criminal liability.

> Eric and Chris completed a domestic partnership declaration, including having their signatures notarized. Eric was employed by a company that offered health benefits to its employees' domestic partners, and Chris took advantage of the health coverage. Later when the relationship ended, Eric discovered that Chris had intentionally not filed the Declaration with the Secretary of State's office.

The law in this case would find no crime under the language of AB 205 since the Declaration was never filed, but Chris certainly is vulnerable to civil and criminal charges of fraud for tricking his partner and the partner's employer into providing medical coverage which was done at a financial expense to both.

Chapter 7

AB 205's Impact on the Workplace

Because there are both federal and state laws relating to employment, there is the probability of confusion about how AB 205 will be applied in the workplace. Many areas raise uncertainties or demonstrate that AB 205 provides rights that are similar but not equal, whether the issues are ones of benefits and family leave or unemployment benefits or nepotism policies.

Benefits

If insurance benefits are offered to married couples, they must now be offered to registered domestic partners. What is more, under legislation signed into law in September 2004, insurance companies must make the benefits that are provided to a domestic partner and the couple's children identical to those provided for married couples and their children.[1] The insurer does have the right to request proof of a registered domestic partnership and notice of termination of the partnership, but if the insurer does so, the same proof and notice must be required for married employees, that is, proof of marriage and notice of dissolution.[2]

AB 205 does not resolve the federal tax implications of these benefits. The Internal Revenue Service has issued several Private Letter Rulings that the receipt of health benefits for one's domestic partner must be considered taxable income to the

---

[1] AB 2208 (Kehoe) creating the California Insurance Equality Act. See Appendix E.

[2] Health and Safety Code section 1374.58(d) [effective January 1, 2005].

employee partner. This means that the value of the benefits is added to the employee's gross taxable income, and federal withholding is based on the higher figure.

> Johnny and Charles are registered domestic partners. Johnny's employer provides health benefits for domestic partners, and Johnny has included Charles on his policy. Johnny's annual income is $50,000. The value of the health benefits for Charles is $300 per month.

The law in this case eliminated this taxation problem as it applied to California residents filing state income tax returns by exempting the value of coverage provided to a domestic partner from the employee partner's gross income,[3] but California laws cannot affect federal tax laws. For federal income tax purposes, Johnny's taxable income is $53,600 (50,000 + ($300 x 12)). While for some couples an employee partner's benefits may be the only ones available, in those cases in which each partner has benefits available, the couple may wish to consider whether they will save federal taxes by each taking his or her own benefits as though they were unmarried persons. It becomes a question of balancing the availability of benefits, the cost of the benefits and the federal taxes on the income attributable to those benefits to make an informed decision.

This tax distinction has ramifications for the employer as well: because an employer's payroll taxes are based on its employees' taxable incomes, when the value of domestic partners' benefits are added to employees' incomes, the employer will pay higher taxes. There is a further administrative burden placed on employers because of this inequitable treatment since the employer will need to maintain separate payroll functions for income tax withholding and for payroll tax.

---

[3] AB 25 (Migden), passed in 2001, modified California Revenue and Taxation Code section 17021.7

Public Employee Benefits

AB 205 prohibits any public agency in the state from discriminating against any individual or couple based on their status as registered domestic partners. The most reasonable interpretation of this law means that AB 205 will require public employers to provide survivor benefits to a surviving domestic partner that are equivalent to those provided to a surviving spouse. This would include offering health and welfare benefits to the same extent that such benefits are offered to spouses.

From the employers' perspectives, it may be necessary to modify or amend their benefit plans to provide for these changes. Some governmental plans may require legislation or voter approval to make such amendments.

AB 25 (Migden), enacted in 2001, provides that, for employees covered by the California Public Employees' Medical and Hospital Care Act (maintained by CalPERS), a domestic partner and a child of a domestic partner will be eligible for continued health care coverage upon the death of the employee or annuitant if the domestic partner is receiving a beneficiary allowance.

Health Benefits

In August 2004, the Legislature passed AB 2208 (Kehoe), the California Insurance Equity for All Families Act, that conforms the laws relating to insurance to the requirements of AB 205. AB 205 does not technically require employers to provide coverage for domestic partners, but it does require employers to provide coverage equal to the coverage that it provides for spouses. Currently, group health plans and insurers are only required to provide coverage for a domestic partner that is equivalent to that offered to a *dependent* of the employee. With AB 2208, insurers must provide coverage that is equal to that offered to an employee's *spouse*. This change to a specific plan does require an application by the employer. These requirements apply to all plans issued, renewed, amended or delivered after January 2,

2005, in California.

It is expected that this new requirement will apply equally to life insurance programs for employees and their spouses or domestic partners. Employers may want to review their various insurance programs in light of AB 2208.

Other Employee Benefits

In addition to providing equal health and welfare benefits, employers will need to offer equal moving expenses, memberships in clubs, membership discounts, travel benefits and any other non-retirement benefit currently offered to an employee's spouse. Whether these are taxable to the employee as income remains to be seen. Most of the benefits probably will fall under the *de minimis* exception under IRS rules for benefits that are of minimal value.

Though AB 205 does not require such changes specifically, if an employer permits leave for the death of a spouse or child, the same leave will need to be permitted for domestic partners.

Cafeteria (Section 125) Plans

An employee partner may be able to add his or her partner to benefits under a Section 125 cafeteria plan that allows the use of pre-tax dollars for the payment of medical and child care expenses. To qualify, the partner or the child must be able to qualify under the IRS rules for defining a dependent for tax purposes.[4]

Family and Medical Leave

Because AB 205 applies all law relating to spouses equally to domestic partners, it affirms that the family and medical leave provisions of the California Family Rights Act (CFRA) are applicable to domestic partners. The CFRA allows up to twelve weeks of unpaid leave to care for the illness of one's spouse,

---

[4] Internal Revenue Code section 152(a).

domestic partner or child. In 2002, SB 1661 (Kuehl) was enacted which created a family temporary disability insurance program that expands the disability insurance program to allow an employee to receive partial wages for up to six weeks of that leave. The paid family care leave under SB 1661 is defined as:

> (1) Leave for reason of the birth of a child of the employee or the employee's domestic partner, the placement of a child with an employee in connection with the adoption or foster care of the child by the employee or domestic partner, or the serious health condition of a child of the employee, spouse or domestic partner.
> (2) Leave to care for a parent, spouse, or domestic partner who has a serious health condition.[5]

SB 1661 clearly intends that Family Temporary Disability Insurance (FTDI) leave must be taken concurrently with leave taken under the FMLA and the CFRA.[6]

> Sarah works for Tykeland Toys. Her partner, Patience, has recently been diagnosed with a serious illness, and Sarah needs to stay home to care for Patience. She applies to her employer and is granted unpaid leave under the California Family Rights Act. She uses the full 12 weeks that are available to her.
>
> Sarah returns to work at Tykeland. Just four months later, Sarah is injured in an auto accident and is hospitalized and then is at home recuperating for eight weeks. How must Tykeland handle her second absence?

The law in this case looks first to the federal Family and Medical Leave Act (FMLA) which, in this situation, does not apply

---

[5] California Unemployment Insurance Code section 3302(b).

[6] California Unemployment Insurance Code section 3303(f).

to an employee who must provide care for a domestic partner. Consequently, the employer would not be able to designate the FMLA leave to run concurrently with the CFRA if it is taken to care for a domestic partner or the child of the partner or of the couple. It appears that Sarah would be entitled, in the example above, to take another eight weeks off under the FMLA for her own serious health problems or any other qualifying event.

Domestic Partnership Status Protected

Because AB 205 has a non-discrimination provision, the Fair Employment and Housing Act (FEHA) will protect domestic partners to the same extent as spouses. Because the FEHA protects against discrimination based on marital status, it is likely to be interpreted to protect an individual based on his or her status as a domestic partner.

Nepotism Policies

Many businesses and agencies have nepotism policies designed to address situations in which two people related by blood or marriage work in the same department or division or office. The concern about nepotism is that one spouse or partner with more authority in the workplace might demonstrate favoritism for the other spouse or partner or might be quick to provide rewards or slow to provide discipline or that the two might form an alliance that affects the working relationships in the office and proves impenetrable by others.

Nepotism policies become more challenging when dealing with gay couples. With employees who are afraid to be out in their workplace, employers may never know a problem exists. Employers must be careful not to discriminate against the employees because of their perceived sexual orientation. On the other hand, if the relationship is public knowledge, the employer may want to look at the language of the nepotism policy and make sure it is worded broadly enough to cover same-sex and opposite-sex relationships equally. If two gay people have formed a domestic partnership, then the company or entity's rules about nepotism should be reviewed because they may now apply to that couple. The law still permits an employer to "reasonably regulate" domestic partners working in the same department, division or facility.[7]

Unemployment Benefits for Relocating With One's Partner

In one of the earlier domestic partner bills, California workers were given the right to apply for unemployment if they had to relocate because their domestic partner had to move elsewhere in the state for work.[8] Unemployment benefits are paid when one involuntarily loses his job, for example, due to layoffs or cutbacks. If a person is fired for misconduct or voluntarily quits, there are usually no benefits available. Quitting a job to relocate is considered voluntary, unless one must do it because his or her spouse has had to move for employment purposes. Although a husband or wife can claim unemployment benefits if his or her spouse must relocate because of work , the same has never been true for same-sex partners. Registered domestic partners now may use this same option.

---

[7] California Government Code section 12940(a)(3)(A).

[8] AB 25 modified sections 1032 and 1256 of the Califomia Unemployment Insurance Code.

Chapter 8

Domestic Partnerships and Property Rights

For many people, discussion of property creates images of things: a television set, a car, clothes, DVDs, and even a house. Property, however, is not always tangible. Property includes such things as credit card debts, bank accounts, retirement benefits, stocks, mineral rights and insurance policies.

Most couples do not pay attention to the nature or character of the property they own. If they acquire it during their marriage, or, under the new law, during their domestic partnership, most people treat the money as theirs jointly. When they take advantage of a sale and buy a new couch, rarely is one of the couple likely to ponder whether this couch is now a community property asset. Typically the character of property is significant when the property must be divided either because of divorce or death. However, it can sometimes be significant during the relationship if, for example, one of the couple becomes liable on a judgment for debts that existed before the marriage or partnership. Judgment creditors in such a situation must look first to collect from the separate property of the responsible individual. Then, that partner's share of community property may also be vulnerable to satisfy the debt.

The Unknown Issues

AB 2580, passed in September 2004, provides that any property determination that requires reference to a date of marriage shall apply to the date of registration for domestic partners, even if that date is prior to January 1, 2005.[9] This means that a couple who registered in January 2002 will be considered to already have been in a domestic partnership for three years in January 2005. This date is relevant for issues such as an award of spousal support, the division of property and, perhaps, regarding children of the couple.

Typically laws that are enacted are prospective only and are not retroactive. This is done because people should be able to make informed decisions at any time about their legal rights. A couple may have made various decisions based on the implications of the then-existing domestic partner law. Now the property and support provisions of AB 205 may apply retroactively to the date the couple registered as domestic partners. Adding another element to the question of retroactivity is the requirement that the Secretary of State must send three separate notices throughout 2004 to registered couples alerting them to the new laws and advising them that they can terminate their partnership prior to January 1, 2005, by filing a simple form signed by just one of the couple. Because registered partners have had such notice and the opportunity to terminate the existing partnership and re-register after January 1, 2005, the retroactivity of the law very well may be upheld since the burden on the couple to terminate their relationship before January 1, 2005, is minimal and termination

---

[9] California Family Code section 297.5(m)(1) defines the law about the date of marriage for domestic partners. The text of that law follows and demonstrates the manner in which attorneys and legislators can string together 116 words in just one sentence:

"For purposes of the statutes, administrative regulations, court rules, government policies, common law, and any other provision or source of law governing the rights, protections, and benefits, and the responsibilities, obligations, and duties of registered domestic partners in this state, as effectuated by this section, with respect to community property, mutual responsibility for debts to third parties, the right in particular circumstances of either partner to seek financial support from the other following the dissolution of the partnership, and other rights and duties as between the partners concerning ownership of property, any reference to the date of a marriage shall be deemed to refer to the date of registration of a domestic partnership with the state."

provides a ready means of protecting pre-existing property rights. Whatever the outcome, the reality is the same: until the courts decide the issue or the Legislature enacts new laws, there is uncertainty, and that uncertainty must be recognized by currently registered couples.

AB 2580 had one other provision that is important in addressing property issues and rights. The bill modified Family Code section 297.5 to give couples until June 30, 2005, to draft and sign an agreement that meets the legal requirements for a premarital agreement.[10] Although typically premarital agreements become effective upon marriage, these agreements will be effective if signed and made effective by June 30, 2005, even though the partners are already registered. This gives the partners another vehicle for handling the problem of the possible retroactivity of the law to the date of registration.

General Obligations Regarding Property

Partners owe an obligation to each other to maintain and protect the joint assets of the couple. The law says that their "...relationship imposes a duty of the highest good faith and fair dealing on each spouse, and neither shall take any unfair advantage of the other."[11] The law considers this a *fiduciary* relationship. The term derives from the same Latin root as the word for fidelity and refers broadly to trust or faith. A fiduciary is typically someone who stands in a confidential relationship with another and has the highest duty to act for the benefit of the other

---

[10] California Family Code section 297.5(m)(2):
Notwithstanding paragraph (1), for domestic partnerships registered with the state before January 1, 2005, an agreement between the domestic partners that the partners intend to be governed by the requirements set forth in Sections 1600 to 1620, inclusive, and which complies with those sections, except for the agreement's effective date, shall be enforceable as provided by Sections 1600 to 1620, inclusive, if that agreement was fully executed and in force as of June 30, 2005.

The full requirements for a premarital agreement are listed in Appendix G.

[11] California Family Code section 721.

person. Attorneys, accountants, registered investment advisors, executors and trustees are examples of the types of individuals who have fiduciary obligations to their clients. The same is true for a husband and wife, and, likewise, the same is now true for registered domestic partners. This means both partners have an obligation to manage and control the community property for the good of the couple.[12]

The fiduciary obligation continues until the relationship is dissolved or until a court makes an order changing this duty. This duty includes the obligation for full disclosure to the other partner of the existence and extent of all community assets and debts and allowing access to such records as may exist about the property. Neither partner may sell, lease for longer than one year, or give away real estate or personal property acquired during the relationship without the written consent or the signature of the other. Additionally, a partner cannot sell or give away or encumber any of the furnishings in the home, property used in the home, or clothing of the other partner or of the children, without the other partner's written consent. This does not mean you each need to sign a written agreement if you intend to have a garage sale with clothes and household items. Such a situation suggests mutual consent. When the property is a business, or an interest in a business, that is substantially community property, the partner who manages the business or business interest has the primary, though not the sole, control or management of the business. The managing partner must give the other partner prior written notice of any major transactions.

The fiduciary obligation is a serious one. Each partner has a claim against the other for any action that impairs the partner's interest in any community property.[13] Mismanagement of the property may subject the offending partner to court action and court orders that will attempt to remedy the harm done to the non-

---

[12] California Family Code section 1100.

[13] California Family Code section 1101.

offending partner.[14]

The spirit of a fiduciary obligation is this: each partner needs to treat the community property appropriately and openly and always act to the benefit of the couple. This includes community property in the form of debts: a partner must not unnecessarily encumber the couple's property or misuse their funds or credit.

Types of Property

Community property. Property in California is in one of two forms: community or separate. In its most simplified form, community property is all property acquired by either party for the duration of the registered domestic partnership that is not separate property. Each partner owns one-half of all community property. This is true even if only one partner worked during the partnership and even if the property is held in the name of only one partner. The property also includes debts incurred during the relationship for which the two are equally responsible.

> Janet works part-time and brings home $800 per month. Jean has a fulltime job with the county and brings home $2200 per month.
>
> Jean recently charged $900 to a credit card in her name alone for an entertainment center. Janet bought new linens and towels for $100 which she charged to their joint credit account.

The law in this case would characterize the $3000 combined earned income each month as community property to which each partner has equal rights. The debts are incurred during the partnership and means the couple shares a community debt of $1000. The linens, towels and entertainment center are all community property as well.

---

[14] California Family Code section 2602.

> During their registered domestic partnership, Donald and Mickey bought and sold various rental properties. Title to two of the properties were put in Donald's name alone. When the couple divorced, Mickey claimed a half interest in the two properties. Donald claimed they were his alone because they were only in his name.

The law in this case presumes that all property acquired during the domestic partnership is community property. A legal presumption puts the burden on the person disagreeing with the characterization of the property to prove that the property is *not* community property. If the person cannot meet that burden of proof, then the property will be considered community. Title to property in the name of just one partner does not overcome the presumption of community property. For community property purposes, which partner acquired the property or earned the income is irrelevant: the property belongs to the community. Community property is created by the earned income of the partners acquired during the course of their registered domestic partnership.

Separate property. Separate property is anything a person had prior to the registered domestic partnership or property acquired during the partnership by gift, inheritance or bequest that the recipient does not convert[15] into community property. Separate property also includes any rents, interest or profits the person makes from the separate property. Separate property is solely within the control of the owner and does not require the consent of the other partner to sell or otherwise transfer the property. If the parties separate in anticipation of dissolving their partnership, income that each partner earns and the debts each partner incurs revert to being separate property in most instances.

Mixed property. The division of property becomes most

---

[15] The legal term is "transmute."

complex when the property is of a mixed character. For example, one partner owns a house before forming a domestic partnership. Because the house was owned prior to the partnership, it is separate property. If, during the relationship, community funds are used to make the house payments or make improvements to the house, there is now a community interest in a portion of the property that must be valued.

> Mary Jane and Carol have been partners for fifteen years. In 2004, they register as domestic partners. In early 2005, Carol's aunt dies and leaves her $25,000.
>
> Example 1: Carol takes the money to the bank, buys a Certificate of Deposit in her name alone, and leaves it there for a year.
>
> Example 2: When Carol went to the bank to buy the CD, she put both her name and Mary Jane's on the CD as joint owners.
>
> Example 3: Carol put the CD in her own name, but made the account Payable on Death (POD) to Mary Jane.
>
> Example 4: Carol leaves the money in the CD. The following year when the certificate matures, Carol rolls $20,000 into a new CD in her name and takes out $5000 which she uses as a down payment for a new vehicle the couple buys together.

The law in this case depends entirely on how Carol treats the money from her aunt, that is, whether she uses it for the community or places it in accounts with other community funds. In the first example above, the CD remains Carol's separate property, as does the interest it earns, and Mary Jane would have no right to it if the couple divorced because Carol has retained the CD in her name and under her sole control. In the second situation, Carol has probably just converted her separate property into community property, and Mary Jane is entitled to half. In the third example, Carol would argue that Mary Jane had no present right to the money and that Mary Jane's name was on the account for estate planning purposes only. In all likelihood, the money would remain Carol's separate property. The fourth example is slightly more complex. The CD would continue to be Carol's separate property, but the money she put into the new vehicle with Mary Jane either could be community property or, depending upon the agreement of the parties, it could still be Carol's separate property for which she would later be entitled to reimbursement if the couple ends their partnership.

A classic example of mixed property is a partner's retirement benefits. To make the math easy, assume Partner A worked for the company for 5 years prior to the domestic partnership. The partners remain together for ten years during which time Partner A continues working at the same company. When the partners separate at the end of ten years, Partner A works for the company 5 more years before retiring. Partner A has worked 5 years + 10 years + 5 years for a total of 20 years. Ten of those years were not during the domestic partnership and are therefore separate property. Another ten years are community property because they accrued during the partnership. Community property means each partner is entitled to half the value of the community interest. As a result, Partner A is entitled to 3/4 (fifteen-twentieths) of the retirement amount, and Partner B is entitled to 1/4 (five-twentieths). Partner B will receive 25% of Partner A's retirement benefits when they are paid.[16]

Debts

Property also includes debts. Just as each member of the couple has a right to a one-half interest in community property, each becomes equally responsible for the community debts that are incurred. Even if a credit card is held in just one partner's name, if the debt is incurred during the partnership, it is a community debt. The exception would be one in which the partners have a pre-relationship agreement that defines debts and

---

[16] The application of AB 205 to federal benefits is discussed later in this chapter.

assets in a different way. For example, the partners might have agreed to treat their respective incomes as separate property even after becoming partners, and they might have decided to treat debts as being the separate property of the one in whose name they are incurred.

Debts which either partner brought into the relationship are the separate debt of that partner. The separate property of a partner is liable for a debt incurred prior to the registered partnership. However, the community property of the couple after registration can be liable for those pre-registration debts.[17] The other partner can protect his or her earnings, which are community property, only if they are kept in a deposit account to which the debtor spouse has no right of withdrawal or are not otherwise commingled.[18] Separate property cannot be made liable for the debt incurred by one's partner before or after registration as domestic partners.[19]

California does have *homestead* laws that allow one or both spouses to declare a house and land as their homestead and thereby protect the house and land against the claims of creditors.[20] The law limits the amount of property that is protected by homestead rights.[21] Since this law applies to spouses, under AB 205, it should apply to homes owned by domestic partners.

Federal Rights and Interests Excluded

The reality that the domestic partner law is not marriage and does not provide equal rights for domestic partners becomes obvious when one attempts to determine how various federal

---

[17] California Family Code section 910.

[18] California Family Code section 911.

[19] California Family Code section 913.

[20] California Code of Civil Procedure section 704.710 et seq.

[21] The amount varies between $50,000 and $150,000 depending upon various circumstances. California Code of Civil Procedure section 704.730.

benefits and entitlements are to be characterized. Again, it is typically not until divorce or death that the character of property becomes actively important, but couples who wish to do estate planning or intend to draft a premarital-type agreement are going to have to confront the issue of how to handle federally-based property.

As an example, under the California Public Employee Retirement System (CalPERS), one can name his or her domestic partner as the recipient of one's retirement benefits. Knowing that such income is available to the couple can be important for retirement or estate planning purposes. Additionally, if the couple were ever to dissolve their relationship, the non-government employee partner would be entitled to one half of the value of the retirement that accrued during their partnership. If the same partner is employed by the federal government instead, it appears that a court would not have the authority to divide the federal benefits as community property and the surviving partner might not be entitled to receive a share of the employee partner's continuing benefits after death. Social Security benefits are not considered community property, but spouses can receive certain derivative benefits such as Social Security based on a former spouse's entitlements. Such derivative rights are not available to domestic partners because their relationships are not recognized federally.

Re-characterizing Property

Because AB 2580 allows registered domestic partners a window of six months, until June 30, 2005, to enter into a written agreement regarding how they will characterize and manage their property, many couples may want to use this time to explore their legal situation and decide whether they wish to re-characterize certain assets and debts. After that date, new partners can still enter into such agreements prior to registering, and post-registration agreements remain an option although the requirements are more specific and exacting since such an agreement seeks to change what has already happened in relation to the property and rights of the parties rather than setting on a prospective agreement about how those matters will be handled.

> Thelma and Louise have lived together in a committed relationship since 1990. They both worked hard, bought a house together, ultimately had enough money to buy a larger house and kept the first one as a rental. They own two cars and an RV. They have a house full of lovely furniture, some of which each had before they met, some inherited from family members in the last dozen years, and a number of items they purchased together. They registered as domestic partners in January 2001.

The law in this case is the kind that makes divorce and estate planning attorneys salivate and creates great test questions for law school professors! The women's property consists of at least four types of property based on the date of purchase or when the property was acquired: pre-relationship, pre-registration, post-registration and post-January 1, 2005. There are numerous non-marital legal issues for the property held prior to registration in terms of determining the ownership interests each may have in the various assets. This couple could benefit from good legal advice and also benefit from drafting a premarital agreement or a post-registration agreement. The premarital agreement must be done before registration or before June 30, 2005, if the couple has registered before that date. The post-registration agreement can be done at any time after registration, but it will be easier to uphold if it is done as soon after registration as possible.

Chapter 9

Domestic Partnerships and Parenting Rights

Before discussing the specifics of custody and adoption, it is worth remembering that historically children have been treated very much like wives, that is, like property. A man owned his children as much as he owned his wife, his cattle and his tools. Although theoretically we are much more sophisticated these days and few people would profess to believe such a thing, there is still that assumption that lies below the surface of most laws. Children belong to their parents, and one cannot alter that relationship without legal intervention.

Gay couples who seek to have children included in the family of their partnership must do so either by means of adoption, artificial insemination or surrogacy. As a result, planning is required. The law has long had a presumption of paternity for any child born while a couple is married. It is assumed that the husband is the father, and he is treated as such unless paternity is disproved. AB 205 does a remarkable thing legally: it applies a parental presumption to registered domestic partners. If one partner gives birth after entering into a domestic partnership, California will treat the other partner as a legal parent of the child.[1] If the couple has a child during the partnership or both adopt a child and later decide to dissolve their relationship, the courts will determine custody and visitation, and both parents will be responsible for support.

---

[1] California Family Code section 297.5(d).

Many legalities remain uncertain about this presumption of parentage. There is already one legal challenge in Virginia based on the parental rights of domestic partners under Vermont's civil union law. Vermont's law is very much like California's and presumes a child born during the relationship is the child of both partners. However, in a case in which the Vermont couple has moved to Virginia, the Commonwealth of Virginia refuses to recognize the non-birth partner's relationship with the child. Because the couple no longer resides in Vermont, the rights they had for their civil union have vanished, and they are again legal strangers. Parents wanting to guarantee the legal relationship with a child from their partnership may still want to explore stepparent adoptions to formalize the parent-child relationship. This is yet another example of the ways in which the rights of domestic partners to be treated like spouses in California are not fully the rights of a married person: they do not extend beyond California's borders, and they do not fit with numerous federal laws and rights. It will be interesting to see what various federal agencies do in these situations. For example, who will be listed as the parents on a child's passport? Will Social Security honor the child's parentage when it comes to children receiving Social Security through their parents?

Stepparent Status

If a domestic partner has a child from a prior relationship or adopted a child prior to the relationship, the child does not automatically become the child of the new domestic partner. Identical to the case for married couples, domestic partners do not take on parental rights for their partner's child from prior relationships nor do they become the child's legal guardian.

Prior to AB 205, a domestic partner had no legal relationship with a partner's child and has had no authority to participate in or make decisions about the child's education, health or other needs. Legally, the domestic partner and the child were strangers. California law does provide authority for a court to award reasonable visitation rights to a stepparent upon divorce if visitation is in the best interest of a child.[2] The same law defines a stepparent as "a person who is a party to the marriage that is the subject of the proceeding, with respect to a minor child of the other party to the marriage."[3] AB 205 addresses any possible problem by confirming that the rights of each of them to any child of the relationship shall be like those of a child of married spouses.[4] Consequently, if one partner has a child prior to the partnership, the new domestic partner shall be treated with the same rights as a stepparent.

Medical Reproduction Technology

As a result of medical reproductive technologies, same-sex couples may have a child who is the biological child of at least one of the partners. There are several possibilities for conception and gestation. Two men might have a child together using the sperm from one and, with the consent of the other partner, use a surrogate mother. A female couple could have a child together using a sperm donor with one woman as the birth mother and the other providing consent.[5] A third scenario would have one female partner provide the ovum and the other act as the gestational birth mother with sperm from a donor. The female providing the ovum would have to consent to the artificial insemination of her partner as with the prior two examples. Although in opposite-sex relationships the presumption of paternity may be overcome with a blood test, blood tests cannot be used to challenge parentage if both parties consented to the medical procedure used for conception.[6]

---

[2] California Family Code section 3101(a).

[3] California Family Code section 3101(c)(2).

[4] California Family Code section 297.5(d).

[5] In both of these situations, the consent would be given in accord with California Family Code section 7613(a).

[6] California Family Code section 7541(e)(2), (3).

If the child was conceived or born prior to registration as domestic partners or prior to January 1, 2005, there could remain uncertainty about the legal relationship of the child to the non-birth mother or the non-donor father. One option would be for that partner to do a stepparent adoption to assure the legal relationship. There is some old case authority that suggests that one cannot adopt one's own child, which the child would be presumed to be under AB 205 if born during the relationship. There is also a legal action possible to confirm parentage, but the California Supreme Court has granted review of three lower court cases, each of which held that this law cannot be applied to two parents of the same gender. For now, that avenue is still uncertain.

Adoptions

Prior to the implementation of AB 205, the laws and regulations varied periodically regarding the ability of either a same-sex couple or an unmarried single person to adopt a child. When adoption by an individual was allowed, he or she often had to create a fiction of being single and without a partner. The child was adopted solely by the one person, and the other partner had no legal rights to the child. Just as if the child were the biological child of one partner from a prior relationship, the other partner had no parental rights if the couple ended their relationship. In fact, the law was such that there was no method available for even bringing the issue before the courts. This is no longer the case under AB 205.

Ultimately judges began accepting the idea of a second-parent adoption, but, at first, it was a matter of finding a sympathetic jurist in a particular county. In some counties, there were no second-parent adoptions. Typically when one adopts a child, the biological parents have to give up all rights to the child. The idea of the second-parent approach was not to take away the rights of the one parent but rather to give the child a second parent. The same rationale had been used for stepparent adoptions by allowing the stepparent to adopt without the biological custodial parent giving up rights to the child.

> Pamela and Kimberly had a baby by medical reproductive means. Pamela carried Kimberly's egg, and both consented to a sperm donor. The baby was born before the couple registered as domestic partners.
>
> Milton and Danny have a child whom Danny adopted before he met Milton. Milton and Danny have registered as domestic partners.
>
> Donna and Bobbie are registered domestic partners. Donna has two daughters from an opposite-sex marriage that ended in divorce many years ago. The girls' father has not seen them or provided any child support since Donna left him.

The law in this case should make most second-parent adoptions unnecessary for gay couples now that stepparent adoptions are an option, although some single heterosexual couples might elect to use the second-parent process. Because California does not permit gay couples to marry, stepparent adoptions have been unavailable to gay couples. However, since January 1, 2002, under new rights established by AB 25 (Migden), registered domestic partners have been permitted to adopt their partners' children in the same manner and process as stepparents.[7] This continues to be the case under AB 205. One practical consideration is that the consent of the child's other biological parent may be required for the stepparent adoption. Because same-sex relationships are often a source of discomfort for some people, especially if they have been married to a person who later comes out as gay, obtaining this consent may be difficult. One condition supersedes the need for consent from the other birth parent. If, for a period of one year, a birth parent willfully fails to communicate with and to pay for the care, support,

[7] California Family Code sections 8604-8606.

and education of a child when able to do so, the custodial parent alone may be able to provide the consent necessary for a stepparent adoption. In the examples above, each couple would be able to use the stepparent adoption process. There would be no need to use a second-parent adoption process.

Stepparent adoptions are less invasive in one sense than regular or second-parent adoptions since they typically do not require a home study, that is, an inspection and evaluation of the child's living situation. An investigation of the stepparent is still required which usually involves confirming the validity of the marriage, confirming the child's legal status and a criminal or child abuse background check; no court can order the adoption without this report.[8] Also, written postadoption contact agreements are possible that would allow the child to continue to have contact with the other birth parent and other birth relatives, including siblings.[9]

Under AB 205, couples will be able to complete an independent or private adoption jointly, eliminating the expense, delay and inconvenience of having to go through two legal proceedings to adopt one child. Additionally, the child will be the child of both partners from the time of adoption, guaranteeing each partner on-going contact with the child as well as requiring each to provide for the care and support of the child.

Legal Guardians

In everyday conversations, parents are often referred to as a child's *legal guardians*. From a technical standpoint, that is not accurate. A legal guardian is an individual appointed by a court who has responsibility either for the health and welfare of a child (the child's *person*) or for any assets or entitlements for a child (the child's *estate*). Parents are not legal guardians, and they do not need to be appointed legal guardians since, as parents, they

---

[8] California Family Code section 9001.

[9] California Family Code section 8616.5.

already have responsibility for and control of their child.[10]

If a biological or adoptive parent were unable to care for a child due to his own health or legal situation, a stepparent might petition the court to be appointed legal guardian for the child and therefore would be able to continue to care fully for the child. The court determines what specific authority the legal guardian will have in each case. The court will always give preference for the selection of a guardian to an individual who has been nominated by the parent, unless the child has a surviving legal parent who may be entitled to custody. If a biological or adoptive parent wants his or her domestic partner to be appointed in case a legal guardianship is ever required for the child, the nomination can be completed as easily as writing a statement saying, "I appoint [partner's name, address] as the legal guardian for the [person and/or estate] of my child[ren] [name(s)]. If [partner's name] cannot act as guardian, I nominate [alternate's name, address]." The nomination of guardian only needs to be signed and dated by the parent to be valid.

---

[10] The only comparable situation might occur when a parent petitions the court to be appointed *guardian ad litem* for a child. This is a guardian specifically appointed to conduct litigation. Such a role is necessary for a parent to act on behalf of a child in a lawsuit, for example, to sue for damages for injuries the child received in an accident.

Chapter 10

Domestic Partnerships, Estate Planning and Probate

Another legal arena that will create substantial challenges under AB 205 is the area of estate planning and probate. Presuming a couple never needs the authority of a divorce court, at some time they will ultimately be in probate court or dealing with the reality of a partner's death. AB 205 has provided many expanded protections, but lacking the application of federal laws regarding estate and gift taxes, domestic partners do not acquire rights equal to those of married couples. Because the procedural aspects of probate are in state courts, the application of California law will give domestic partners the same rights. The application of estate and gift taxes, both of which are governed by federal laws, will result in very different outcomes for domestic partners, especially for those with estates of higher values.

The fact that AB 205 is a California-only law is critical in considering estate planning and related matters. If registered domestic partners move out of California, the laws that protected some of their rights in California likely will not apply to them in their new state of residence. Estate planning would be necessary. If the couple travels outside the state, and one should have to make medical decisions or end-of-life decisions for the other, those rights may not exist in the locale to which they have traveled. Estate planning would have been necessary. The same might be true about making funeral or burial decisions out of state or even being able to claim the deceased partner's personal effects. While one can count on numerous protections while in

California, the minute the couple leaves the state, they are effectively reduced to legal strangers.

Wills

California has a Statutory Will, that is, a form dictated by the law (statute) that can be used as a Will. With the passage of AB 25 in 2001, domestic partners were allowed to use this form. The form is designed to apply to a broad range of situations and estates, and it is available for a minimal fee at many stationery stores and online. It allows the maker of the Will, the *testator*, to select different provisions that might be applicable to his or her situation. Because it is in a form prescribed by the law, courts will accept it as a valid Will if it has been filled out according to the instructions. There is only one California Statutory Will form.[11]

The Statutory Will is useful for many people, but it does have limitations. The form itself provides question and answer information and cautions that it is not the appropriate method for estate planning in various circumstances. A specifically drafted Will would be preferable when any of the following conditions exist:

- the value of the estate exceeds the estate and gift tax limit
- one owns business-related assets
- the individual wants to create a trust for a child's education or other purposes
- one owns assets in another state
- the individual wishes to disinherit a domestic partner or others who might typically receive something from the person's estate
- the individual has valuable interests in profit-sharing or pension plans.[12]

Obviously one can attempt to write his or her own Will or

---

[11] California Probate Code section 6223.

[12] California Probate Code section 6240.

can use the services of an estate planning attorney. One can even use a holographic Will, that is, one written in the individual's own handwriting, signed and dated.[13] Perhaps the most important thing is keeping one's Will current when there have been major life changes such as becoming registered domestic partners, the dissolution or annulment or termination of a domestic partnership, the birth or adoption of a child, or if there is a major change in the value of assets.

Wills become especially important for gay couples, largely because the typical pattern of inheritance that is true for most married couples does not necessarily apply for domestic partners. In many marriages, the expectation is that if one spouse dies, the property will go to the other spouse, especially if there are any children. If both spouses should die, again, most typically, they want to benefit their children. Because many gay couples do not have children and because many have strained familial relationships because of their sexual orientation, many couples may want to provide thoughtful direction about who will receive their estates upon death.

> Betty and Wilma are registered domestic partners. Betty's parents are deceased, and she has one sibling with whom she is very close. Wilma was an only child and has a first cousin as her only surviving relative, although they are not particularly close and have not seen each other in years. The two partners have about $750,000 each in separate property assets, and they own another $200,000 in community property. Do they need Wills?

The law in this case is such that both partners would want to have Wills. The community property will pass to the surviving partner on death, but they each have substantial separate property. Under laws relating to the determination of who inherits when a person dies without a Will, half of each

[13] California Probate Code section 6111. Dating the document is very important.

partner's separate property would go to the surviving partner, but the other half would go to the surviving relatives, that is, Betty's sibling and Wilma's cousin. Wills also would allow the partners to divide their estates in alternate ways if their partner did not survive. For example, Wilma might not want to leave things to her cousin but might want to leave things to Betty's sister or to a favorite charity. These outcomes can only be assured with a well-drafted Will.

Joint Tenancy

The use of joint tenancy as a means for holding the title to real property has been used by many people to avoid the need for Wills. Joint tenancy gives an automatic right of survivorship to the surviving partner when one partner dies. This becomes an attractive proposition if one is worried about family members challenging a Will, although, in fact, legal challenges to Wills are difficult and expensive and do not occur as frequently as do the fears of people that they *might* happen. Often couples will not bother to draft Wills if their primary asset, their real property, is held in joint tenancy. This can be a serious shortcoming.

There are a number of reasons that joint tenancy is not the best option for domestic partners. There may be issues of taxability related to the creation of joint tenancies as gifts, the reassessment of the property for taxes on the death of the original joint tenant and the problem with stepping up basis upon death.[14] The most significant problem with holding title as joint tenants is the lack of a contingent beneficiary when one dies and the other partner dies shortly thereafter. The function of joint tenancy is such that when one joint tenant dies, the ownership of the entire property immediately transfers to the surviving tenant.

---

[14] The problem of basis is discussed in more detail later in this chapter. Basis is the cost of a property when calculating capital gains.

> Kendra and Yvonne are registered domestic partners. They have no children. Neither of their families were particularly pleased to know they are lesbians nor are the families happy about the domestic partnership. The two own a nice house that they purchased together, and, to avoid any trouble from their families, they hold title as joint tenants. The house is worth about $500,000, and they only owe $100,000 on the mortgage. Sadly, the two are in a serious auto accident and Kendra is killed instantly. Yvonne survives for several days before she succumbs to her injuries. Who owns the house?

The law in this case creates a survivor-takes-all situation and effectively disinherits Kendra's family. At the moment of Kendra's death, Yvonne became the owner of the entire interest in the house. Although this may be what Kendra wanted, that is, for Yvonne to have the house, because Yvonne died shortly thereafter, the share that Kendra contributed will now go to Yvonne's heirs. If Kendra had heirs or even friends or charities that she wanted to have her $200,000 share, that will not happen. Yvonne's family will get the house. If couples have property of any substantial value, they may want to get legal advice before they take title to property, and they should make the decision about how title is held part of planned and considered estate planning.

Inheritance Under a Will

When a person dies,[15] if the individual has a Will, then the property of that person will be distributed as directed by the Will. The person who writes a Will nominates an *Executor*, that is, a person who will go to the court to have the will probated and who will carry out or *execute* the provisions of the Will. The *testator* may have relieved the Executor of posting a bond which is intended to guarantee that the Executor will not misuse or divert

---

[15] The person who has died is referred to as the *decedent*. When a decedent writes a Will, he or she is also referred to as a *testator*.

any of the assets of the estate.

Many people try to avoid probate, believing it to be an expensive process. The law sets the fees that can be charged by both the executor and the attorney for the estate. These fees are based on a percentage of the value of the estate. For example, the ordinary fees for an estate valued at $250,000 would be $8000. For an estate of $1,000,000, the fees would be $23,000. The court can order additional fees paid if the assets are particularly complex or if the estate requires further legal services beyond those that are typical of a probate.

Inheritance Without a Will

Not uncommonly, people die without making a Will or without doing other estate planning. When there is no Will, the law dictates who will receive the person's property. The law has an order in which the property is distributed.[16] Upon death, one half of the community property belongs to the surviving spouse and the other half to the decedent.[17] Under AB 205, property acquired during the domestic partnership will be considered community property. As a result, the law dividing the community property on death will apply to domestic partners. If a person dies without a Will, the surviving partner will receive the deceased partner's half of the community property, giving the surviving party all the community property of the couple.[18] If the decedent also had separate property, then its division depends upon whether any members of his or her family survive in addition to the domestic partner. If the person dies with no surviving children, parents, siblings or children of the siblings, then all the separate property goes to the surviving domestic partner.[19] If the decedent dies with only one child or their offspring or with no children but with one or

---

[16] The term for this order of distribution is *intestate succession.*

[17] California Probate Code section 100.

[18] California Probate Code section 6401.

[19] California Probate Code section 6401(c)(1).

both parents or a sibling or the sibling's offspring living, then the surviving partner receives one half of the separate property and the other half is divided among the other survivors.[20] A third of the separate property goes to the surviving partner and the other two-thirds is divided if the decedent leaves more than one child, leaves one child and the offspring of one or more deceased child or if the decedent leaves offspring of two or more deceased children.[21] The division of these assets to others besides the surviving domestic partner becomes much more complex and are beyond the scope of this book.[22] Additionally, there are numerous other variables that make it worthwhile to have a consultation with a good probate attorney, especially if there is separate property and if there are other potential survivors.

An individual who dies without a Will is said to have died *intestate*. If there is no Will, the court must appoint someone to handle the estate. Rather than being called an executor, the person who will handle the probate of this estate is called an *administrator*. Typically a court will require an administrator to post a bond of some set value. The same probate fees that apply to estates with Wills apply to those administered without a Will.

Estates Not Requiring Probate

The probate laws allow the transfer of an estate with a value not greater than $100,000 without the formal probate process.[23] This applies even if the decedent owns real property, as long as the total dollar amount is not exceeded. In these cases, an affidavit is drafted that recites certain facts about the decedent and the property involved, identifies the individual(s) entitled to receive the estate and attaches a certified copy of the death certificate. The law is somewhat generous in excluding

---

[20] California Probate Code section 6401(c)(2).

[21] California Probate Code section 6401(c)(3).

[22] California Probate Code section 6402.

[23] California Probate Code section 13100.

certain property from the dollar total, such as automobiles, boats, motor homes and manufactured homes as well as certain bank accounts and up to $5,000 in unpaid salary and vacation leave.

The law defines the successors to the estate in the same way as it does when a person dies without a Will. Consequently, one's domestic partner would be in first position to inherit the deceased partner's estate. This option is helpful in handling modest estates since it avoids probate and court fees entirely.

Inclusion Rules

When a person dies, the federal government becomes interested in the property transferred because the transfers can create taxable situations, although spouses are typically shielded from many such consequences. This is not likely to be so for same-sex couples. The issue is determining what property is included in one's estate for purposes of estate taxes or for capital gains when the property later is sold. If a same-sex couple holds property in joint tenancy, the full value of the joint tenancy property is included in the deceased joint tenant's estate unless the survivor can prove contribution. For spouses, there is a presumption that each contributed equally so only half the value of the property is attributed to the deceased spouse.

In practical terms, this means that the full value of property is attributable to the deceased partner unless the surviving partner can prove that he or she contributed some portion to the purchase of the property. If the couple owns considerable real estate, for example, this could push the value of the deceased partner's estate over the minimum limit for estate taxes. Estate taxes are payable on estates over $1,500,000, and, at a maximum, the rate payable is 48%.[24] If most of the value of the estate is in a home or other real estate, the estate might not have sufficient cash to pay the estate taxes, possibly forcing the sale of property to obtain

---

[24] These are the estate tax exemptions and rates for 2004. The dollar limit stays the same for 2005, and the maximum rate drops a whopping 1% to 47%. The exemption amount increases to $2,000,000 in 2006.

sufficient funds.

Another inequity of this situation is that if the full value is attributed to one partner and the survivor inherits the property, the full value of the property will again be attributed to the second partner's estate and perhaps cause estate taxes to be due again. Instead of recognizing that each has a half, because they are not married, each one's estate will be taxed fully on the entire value, thus doubling the payment of taxes on the same property!

Basis

A related issue is the question of basis. The basis for a property is usually the value one has paid for the property, in cash, debt obligations, other property or services. Basis can be adjusted up or down by various events. Typically improvements to a property will increase the basis in the property. The improvements must be permanent such as remodeling, not just painting or repairs. When the property is sold, the question becomes one of whether the owner has made money, which is a capital gain, or lost money, which is a capital loss. However, when a person dies, the value of his or her share of an asset, in most instances, is considered to be the fair market value of the asset at the time of death.[25] In California, a spouse receives a step-up in basis for both the decedent's share of the community property as well as for his or her own share of community property. The result is that there is no capital gain if the surviving spouse chooses to sell the property then.

---

[25] There are a number of other ways of establishing basis, so you may need to consult an attorney or accountant for help if this is a potential issue for you.

Example 1: Ed and Hazel are husband and wife. They bought a rental property in 1985 for $50,000. When Hazel died in 2000, the rental was worth $350,000. In 1995, they had added a second floor to the rental for $100,000.

Example 2: Using the same scenario as above, instead we are talking about Rick and Curt who are registered domestic partners.

The law in this case depends entirely on the marital status of the couples. In the first example, the basis is $150,000 ($50,000 cost + $100,000 capital improvements). If the couple had sold the rental in 1998 for $300,000, there would have been $150,000 capital gain. Because they did not sell it, Ed inherits the rental property from Hazel at her death. The basis for the property is stepped-up to $350,000. If Ed decides to sell the property several years later for $400,000, he will only pay capital gains on $50,000 ($400,000 sales price - $350,000 stepped-up basis = $50,000 gain). In the second example, even though the property is considered community property in California, only Curt's half of the property is increased to the fair market value at his date of death. Rick's share is unchanged. They each have an initial $75,000 basis in the rental due to the cost and improvements. The value of Curt's half is increased to the date of death value, which would be $175,000. Rick's half is unchanged, and his basis remains $75,000 for a total of $250,000 for the whole property. When Rick sells the property the next year for $400,000, he has a $150,000 capital gain on which he will have to pay taxes.

Gift Taxes

At death, an estate must be reconciled with the federal government. As discussed above, estate and gift taxes are due for estates of $1,500,000 or more. Part of the reconciliation for taxes is a report of gifts the decedent made during his or her lifetime that were not subject to an annual exclusion amount, were not made to a qualified charitable organization or were not made to a spouse. Each year one can give up to $11,000 to another individual without gift tax consequences. Transfers to a spouse, when made in a qualified manner, are not included in the determination of a taxable gift or a taxable estate. The same is not true for domestic partners. Partners may still gift up to $11,000 per year to each other under general gift exemptions, but no spousal-like exemptions apply.

The gift tax issue is a serious one because of the uncertainty about the manner in which various community property issues between domestic partners may create gift tax consequences. There are considerable unknowns about the treatment of community property income. AB 205 states that "Earned income may not be treated as community property for state income tax purposes."[26] For federal income taxes, community earned income is split between the parties. This is usually irrelevant for married couples since they typically file joint federal income tax returns. Domestic partners are unable to file joint federal or state returns, so, under the Internal Revenue Code, each domestic partner would presumably be expected to report half of the community income on his or her tax return. However, AB 205 says earned income cannot be treated as community property for *state* income tax purposes. The outcome is either that the income is split for federal taxes but not for state taxes or income is reportable only by the earning partner for both federal and state income taxes. If the split-income interpretation prevails, then the next issue is whether this will be considered a gift of one-half the amount to a non-earning partner. If the interpretation is that earned income is not community property for either state or federal income tax purposes, then another possible gift tax problem arises. In this latter situation, because the earning partner would be required to report all his earned income, the implication is that the income is the separate property of the earning partner. If the income is separate, how is it that the

---

[26] California Family Code section 297.5(g).

property purchased by this separate property taxable income becomes community property? Conversion, or transmutation, of separate property into community property creates a gift for federal gift tax purposes. Does this mean that a gift occurs each time one receives a paycheck? Are there mutual gifts if each partner has an income or are the two amounts added together and only the excess of the higher wage earner's salary is deemed a transfer to the lower wage earner?

By now your eyes have either glazed over, you have decided to go to law school or you have new appreciation for attorneys. Whatever your reaction, the message is clear: with all the rights domestic partners have obtained under AB 205, because this is not *marriage*, there will be unresolved legal issues that could take years to sort out.

Powers of Attorney

Powers of attorney are documents which allow one individual to give another person the power to make various decisions in certain situations. The person giving the authority is referred to as the *principal*. The person who is given the authority to act is referred to as an *agent* for health care decisions or as an *attorney-in-fact* for handling financial matters. The person who is selected does not need to be an attorney at law to have this authority. Powers of attorney can be broad in scope or can be limited in the authority they grant. California law allows the drafting of *durable* powers of attorney. What makes them durable is that they survive the incompetency and even the death of the principal. Typically, a power of attorney becomes invalid when the principal becomes incompetent. The rationale for the durable powers of attorney is to have a document that will actually be useful or go into effect when one needs it most, that is, when the principal is incapacitated and needs someone to be able to make decisions about personal care or business affairs. In many instances, a durable power of attorney can prevent the expense of petitioning the court for the appointment of a conservator for the person. California has prescribed statutory forms for powers of attorney that can be used, or a person can have one drafted to confer very specific authority.

Because AB 205's effect is limited to the State of California, most domestic partners will want to have powers of attorney, especially for health care decisions, in the event they travel outside the state. There is no guarantee that another state will accept the document, but many states will, and without such documents, the partners are again reduced to being legal strangers to each other.

Conservatorships

One might not think the topic of conservatorships belongs in a chapter such as this, but it is the probate court that handles conservatorships, and the relevant law is in the Probate Code.[27] A conservator can be appointed for the person or estate of an individual, that is, to oversee one's physical welfare or to manage one's assets. Conservators are appointed only when a person cannot adequately care for himself.[28] Preference in the appointment of a conservator is given to one's spouse or domestic partner. If the spousal or partner cannot serve, the court has an order of priority in appointment that it follows: an adult child, then a parent and then an adult sibling.[29] The priority status of a domestic partner to appointment as conservator minimizes the possibility that a family member who is not friendly to the couple can gain legal authority and undermine or negate the wishes of the couple. An appointment of a conservator can be temporary and is always subject to review by the court.

There is a well-known story, particularly poignant to gay and lesbian people, about Sharon Kowalski who was badly injured and almost killed in an auto accident in 1983 in Minnesota. She

[27] Guardianships are also handled by the probate court.

[28] California Probate Code section 1801.

[29] California Probate Code section 1812.

had lived with her partner Karen Thompson for many years, but neither woman had come out to their families. Upon learning of the accident, Karen immediately went to the hospital, but she was denied any information because she was not a family member. She could not even learn whether her partner was alive or dead. When Sharon's family arrived, Karen was able to learn that Sharon had suffered brain damage and was left a quadriplegic by the accident. Sharon's father learned the nature of the women's relationship, and declaring Karen to be an "animal," he moved Sharon away from the area where the women had lived and prohibited visits from Karen. It took four years for Karen to get a court order to have Sharon examined to see if she was able to express her wishes about seeing Karen. When it was established that Sharon wanted to see Karen, visitation was arranged. It had been five years since the accident. When Sharon's father had to step down as conservator because of his health, despite supportive testimony from Sharon's caregivers that Karen was best suited to care for Sharon, the court appointed a virtual stranger to the role. It took two more years before an appellate court finally stated the obvious: Karen was the best person to care for Sharon, and it was Karen who Sharon wanted as her caretaker. After almost nine years, Sharon came home, and Karen has given that care without the legal and social benefits that are typically available for families in similar situations.

Trusts

The subject of trusts is extraordinarily complex in many respects. While putting assets in trust can avoid the necessity of probate, there are numerous technicalities that must be addressed to make the trust achieve its intended purposes. A trust can be an effective vehicle in estate planning, although much of its value depends upon the terms of the trust being followed exactly. It is also necessary to make sure that all designated property is put into the trust. Otherwise, one can be left with a trust in order to disburse some assets and, additionally, the need to probate other assets that were left out of the trust.

There are a number of different kinds of trusts. An individual trust should not be affected by AB 205, though there may be some questions about funding the trust with a partner's half of community property, since both partners are entitled to equal control and management of community assets. Joint trusts between same-sex partners were, and remain, of uncertain value because transfers into the joint trust may transmute separate property into community property and create gifts to the other partner which most likely will be considered a completed taxable gift. There may be other gift tax consequences, too, depending upon the property used to fund the trust. Generation Skipping Transfer Trusts should not be impacted, though one must use non-family generation assignment rules when planning for transfers to the relatives of one's domestic partner.

The Safekeeping of Legal Documents

When it comes to same-sex couples, it has always been considered good practice for the couple to keep their documents someplace that is safe from an upset family member who might destroy them. For non-gay readers, such advice sounds harsh and perhaps suspicious, but family members have been known to destroy a Will or a nomination of guardianship or conservatorship because that relative knew that the same-sex partner has no legal recourse or standing. It is an unfortunate fact of life for some gay people that families can be intolerant. The possibility of having one's wishes negated are less likely with AB 205 and the legal presumptions and priorities it confers. Although families appear to have less conflict than they had twenty years ago, the issue of the safety of one's documents always should be addressed. Many will elect to leave documents with their attorneys, knowing that the documents will be released only to the proper person or filed with the court and are, therefore, safe.

Chapter 11

Terminating a Domestic Partnership: Summary Termination

The process for terminating a domestic partnership depends on the length of time that has passed since the couple registered, whether the couple owns any real property[1] and whether they have any children. For many couples, ending their domestic partnership will now require filing a petition for dissolution in the local superior court and, possibly, the expense of attorneys to represent each partner.[2] However, just as for opposite-sex couples, the law allows a summary or more expedited termination if the couple meets specific criteria. The summary process allows filing of a Notice of Termination of Domestic Partnership with the Secretary of State without filing a superior court action for dissolution of the domestic partnership.

Signature of Both Parties

Prior to January 1, 2005, one partner could unilaterally terminate the domestic partnership by completing a form, having

---

[1] Real property is typically real estate: a house, condominium or land that one owns or is buying. An interest in real property can include rights other than ownership rights, such as a lease or an option to buy. All other property is personal property: cars, furniture, computers, bank accounts, stocks, retirement plans, annuities and the like.

[2] Attorneys will not represent both parties jointly because that creates a conflict of interest that violates ethical standards. In such situations, to advocate something for one client may mean taking something away from the other client, putting the attorney in a conflict. Each attorney has an obligation for protecting one client's rights.

his or her signature notarized and filing the form with the Secretary of State. Both parties will now have to sign the Notice of Termination of Domestic Partnership.

No Children

The summary termination process is available only if there are no children of the relationship between the domestic partners born before or after registration of the partnership. Likewise, there can be no children adopted by the parties after registration, and neither domestic partner, to their knowledge, can be pregnant at the time of termination.

Length of Partnership

The couple may have lived together previously, but for a summary termination, the couple has to have been registered partners for fewer than five years. The time is calculated from the date the partnership was registered to the date the Notice of Termination is filed.[3]

> Frank and Ernie moved in together on August 1, 2002. On January 3, 2005, they registered with the Secretary of State as domestic partners. On December 5, 2009, Ernie moved out. They had no children, no real estate, no leases and otherwise met the requirements for summary dissolution. Ernie had an auto accident and was hospitalized for two weeks in late December. They did not file to terminate their partnership until January 10, 2010.

The law in this case means Frank and Ernie will have to

---

[3] California Family Code section 2400(a)(4) governing summary dissolutions for opposite-sex marriage says that the marriage cannot be "... more than five years in duration *at the time the petition is filed.*" [emphasis added] Family Code section 299(a)(3) says that the domestic partnership cannot be "more than five years in duration." Because the summary process for domestic partnerships mirrors that for summary dissolution of a marriage, the couple should calculate the five-year period from the date they registered to the date they file the Notice of Termination. Additionally, AB 2580 defines *date of marriage* for domestic partnerships as the date of registration.

file in Superior Court to terminate their relationship because their registered domestic partnership is more than five years in duration. They had to file within five years of the date of registration. In this example, they missed the cut-off point by one week. For deadlines such as these, the law is not flexible and legal deadlines are absolute, regardless of the justification for missing the date.

No Real Property or Lease Longer Than One Year

The summary termination law is not available if either partner has any interest in real property, wherever that property might be located. This applies even if the property was owned before the couple registered. Because it is conceivable that one partner could acquire a community property interest in the property of the other partner, and because the owner of the property could have handled the property in such a manner that requires reimbursement to the non-owning partner, the authority of the Superior Court would be required to establish the partners' respective rights.

The interest in real property can also be a lease for the residence that either party occupies. However, if the lease terminates within one year from the date of filing the Notice of Termination and does not include an option to purchase property, the couple can still qualify for the summary termination process.

Limit on Debts

On January 1 of each odd-numbered year, the California Judicial Council adjusts the dollar amount of debts and property that a couple can own and still qualify for a summary dissolution of marriage. Those same dollar amounts apply to determine whether a couple qualifies for a summary termination of their domestic partnership. As of January 1, 2003, there cannot be unpaid obligations, excluding any debt for an automobile, incurred by either or both of the parties after registration of their domestic partnership in excess of $4,000.00.

Community Property Value

Property or income acquired by either of the parties during the domestic partnership other than by gift or inheritance is generally considered community property. Just as with the debts, the Judicial Council biannually adjusts the maximum value of property which the couple can own and still qualify for summary dissolution or termination. The value does not include automobiles, and any encumbrance or remaining indebtedness on the property is excluded in determining its value. Deferred compensation and retirement plans acquired during the partnership are included. The same maximum allowable value is placed on each partner's separate property assets, that is, the value of property the partner owned prior to the registered partnership or acquired during the partnership by gift or inheritance. The dollar limit for both of those amounts as of January 1, 2003, was $32,000.

> When Patience and Sarah became registered domestic partners, Sarah owned a small cabin at Lake Tahoe that was worth $85,000. The two used the cabin and made some repairs to the roof last year. After four years, the two decided to terminate their domestic partnership. Sarah and Patience had shared an apartment in Oakland on which they had eleven months remaining on a one-year lease.

The law in this case would not allow the couple to do a summary termination because Sarah owns an interest in real property. There is also a question of possible contributions made from the community funds of the two women to Sarah's separate property. The lease would not otherwise have prevented them from using the summary process.

> When Wyatt and Doc became domestic partners, they each owned a car on which they were making payments. Other than their cars, they had a large screen television and a number of appliances and several rooms of furniture that they had purchased together. Those items had a current fair market value of $5,000, but they still owed $1,500 on them, giving the property a net value of $3,500. They own a boat worth $8,000. Wyatt had earned $12,000 in a deferred compensation plan through his job, and Doc had earned slightly more than $6,000 toward his retirement. Wyatt also had a $10,000 certificate of deposit that his grandmother gave him last year on his 25th birthday.

The law in this case would allow summary dissolution by the two domestic partners. The total indebtedness of the couple is $1,500, which is under the $4,000 limit. The combined value of the community property they own is $29,500 ($3,500 + $8,000 + $12,000 + $6,000), which is under the $32,000 limit. The autos and the loans on the autos are excluded from the calculations. In addition, Wyatt's certificate of deposit, which is his separate property because he acquired it as a gift, does not exceed the $32,000 limit for separate property.

The Partners Have a Written Agreement and Have Signed All Necessary Documents[4]

One of the criteria for a summary termination is the requirement that the parties sign a written agreement that specifies how they will divide assets and debts and that they sign necessary documents, such as certificates of title or bills of sale, that are required to put the agreement into effect. There is nothing that requires the agreement be written by an attorney if the partners believe they can write a clear document that defines their agreement.

The agreement should include a statement confirming that each has waived spousal support and that each has read a

[4] See Appendix F for a sample Termination Agreement.

Secretary of State brochure about termination. There is no requirement that the partners' signatures must be notarized or that the document is witnessed. As with any valid legal document, the partners should show the date on which they signed their agreement.

Each Partner Waives Spousal Support

Another of the conditions that must be met for a couple to use the summary termination procedure is that each partner must waive the right to claim spousal support from the other. The waiver is permanent, and, even if situations change drastically after the termination, once the support has been waived, the partner cannot go back and request it. This is a decision that must be undertaken with serious thought.

Typically when two people have not been together for very long, a court would award minimal support or at least would not order support for any significant duration. For that reason, the decision may be easier to make. The factors the partners would want to weigh are the length of the relationship, which would have to be under five years to use this summary process, and the relative income of the two partners. If one partner had a monthly income of $4000 and the other an income of $1500, it might be worth the lower-paid partner seeking support through the judicial process. However, there needs to be a cost-benefit consideration before one decides to seek support. By contrast, if this were a married couple, assume that the lower-income spouse hoped to get $1000 per month as spousal support. Any spousal support is taxable to the person who receives it. Immediately the recipient spouse's income would be considered to be $2500 per month, and he would owe taxes on that amount. If he did not withhold enough taxes to cover the added income, there could be tax penalties. Otherwise, he would need to make quarterly estimated tax payments on the additional $1000 per month. Because this is a same-sex couple, the tax deductibility rules do not apply.[5] Determining a reasonable amount for spousal support and the resulting tax consequences can become much more complicated.

While some people can represent themselves in court, the details of the dissolution process have become so complex in recent years that most people will need to hire an attorney. The cost for an attorney easily can range from $200 to $500 per hour throughout California. Attorneys are paid by the hour, and a complex case can be long and costly, upsetting and irrational. Once the court process begins, costs become a realistic factor, and, even though the end of the relationship may be very emotional, there are practical financial considerations that cannot be ignored in the process. My former law partner took her first divorce case many years ago: a couple who had been married eight months. They soon began arguing over which one was entitled to the Christmas tree lights in the division of property. The lights probably cost less than $20 when new. As the attorney fees built and built, so did my partner's resolve never to practice family law. She later became a very successful estate planning attorney. In my own practice a number of years ago, I sat in four days of meetings with my client, the wife, her soon-to-be former husband and his attorney. Between the two attorneys, these conferences were probably costing about $500 per hour. Both attorneys had urged the clients to make a reasonable estimate of the value of their property rather than paying fees to argue about items of minimal value. We four sat going through numerous reference books trying to value some of the small items of personal property. I remember most vividly the argument about the value of the four ice cream scoops the couple owned. My client died unexpectedly four months after the divorce of natural but unknown causes.

---

[5] See Chapter 12 for a more thorough discussion of the issue of spousal support.

The Parties Have Read and Understand Information on the Termination Process

The Secretary of State must provide a brochure that will be available to all domestic partners who are contemplating terminating their partnership. The brochure will give basic information on the requirements, nature, and effect of terminating a domestic partnership. The written agreement of the partners should include a statement that each partner confirms that he or she has read the brochure and understands its contents.

Both Partners Want the Termination

One more condition for this summary process is that both parties want the termination. The Notice of Termination of Domestic Partnership will also state that fact, but it would be good practice to include a statement to that effect in the written agreement as well.

Because California is a no-fault state when it comes to dissolution of marriage, and because the domestic partnership dissolution will parallel that for married couples, there is no way in California to prevent the dissolution of a marriage or, now, a domestic partnership. Even if one partner objects to the termination, his or her refusal only means that the summary process cannot be used and the couple will be required to go to court. If one wants to terminate the partnership legally, the other partner may make it difficult or expensive, but one will never be able to prevent the relationship from being legally ended.

Six-Month Waiting Period Required

From the date a couple files a Notice of Termination of Domestic Partnership, there is a six-month waiting period before the termination is final. During that six-month period, neither party may legally enter into another registered domestic partnership nor may either partner marry another person. Should the time come that same-sex marriages are legal in California, the gay couple would not need to terminate their domestic partnership before marrying each other. However, they could not legally marry another person until terminating their existing partnership and waiting for the six months to pass.

During this six-month period, either party has the right to file with the Secretary of State a notice of revocation of the termination of the domestic partnership. If a partner files such notice, a copy of the notice must be sent by first class mail, postage prepaid, to the other partner at his or her last known address. If the notice of revocation of the termination is filed because the partners have reconciled, then no further action is needed and the partnership continues legally. If a revocation is filed to prevent the summary termination but the relationship ends nonetheless, the couple must either begin the summary process again, if it is still within the first five years, or one partner will have to file an action in superior court for dissolution of the partnership.

If neither party revokes the termination, at the end of the six-month period, each partner is legally free to enter into another registered domestic partnership or to marry. The summary termination is treated in all respects as the entry of a judgment of summary dissolution.

Setting Aside the Summary Termination

Either partner has the right to file a superior court action for dissolution of the partnership and to set aside the summary termination if the partner can prove fraud, duress, mistake or any other legally recognized basis for setting aside a judgment. With sufficient proof, the court has the authority to set aside the termination and declare it null and void if the parties did not meet the requirements at the time they filed the Notice of Termination of Domestic Partnership. Therefore, if the partners decide to use the summary process and manipulate the figures or overlook certain things that would otherwise have disqualified them from using the summary procedure, then both partners have committed fraud. One partner may have concealed certain information from the other partner about assets. This, too, could be fraud that could justify setting aside the summary termination. Duress is more difficult to prove.[6] The objecting partner would have to convince the court that his or her partner had applied such pressure that the alleged consent was the result of fear or threats. A mistake can be either about the law or a fact. For example, the partners might have filed for summary termination under the mistaken belief about the value of certain of their assets or about whether certain retirement accounts were to be included in the valuation. A mistake can also occur when it is made by one partner and the other partner is aware of the mistake but takes no action to correct the error or bring it to the other person's attention.

The Importance of Compliance

Why would a partner want to go to the expense of setting aside the summary termination and forcing the couple into court? Why not just let it slide if neither partner cares? The short answer is: if the summary termination is not legal, any subsequent partnership or marriage would not be legal either.

Why even include a comment like this? Is it not obvious that one must complete the legal process fully? The answer goes back to earlier comments: people in the gay community have not had the experience of having legally binding relationships. Too often, gay people have had to create relationships and connections and legal arrangements that approximate marriage or at least maximize their rights in relation to each other. However, these arrangements were often informal and thus easily disposable. In addition, there are domestic partners who registered to take advantage of the minimal protections available

---

[6] California Civil Code section 1569 states that duress consists of: 1) unlawful confinement of the person of the party, or the husband or wife of such party, or of an ancestor, descendent, or adopted child of such party, husband, or wife; 2) unlawful detention of the property of any such person; or 3) confinement of such person, lawful in form, but fraudulently obtained, or fraudulently made unjustly harassing or oppressive.

prior to January 1, 2005, and who may now realize how legally bound they are to each other and wish to disregard the legal bond of the relationship if not the relationship itself.

Chapter 12

Terminating a Domestic Partnership: Dissolution, Legal Separation and Nullity

Just as with the termination of opposite-sex marriages, there will be three ways of ending domestic partnerships that do not qualify for summary termination procedures: dissolution, legal separation and nullity. The grounds for dissolution and legal separation are the same. The grounds for a nullity are more varied, but specifically limited. The outcome of each is different. This will be a substantial change to the options same-sex couples have had previously. Before January 1, 2005, any property dispute between partners had to be settled in a civil lawsuit, either in the vein of the dissolution of a business partnership between co-owners or by using what is referred to as a *Marvin* action, that is, a lawsuit based on the breach of an implied agreement between the two individuals regarding property and support.[1] There were many difficulties with such suits, the least of which was that they were based on contract law and often took months to come to trial. On January 1, 2005, domestic partners will use the family law courts of the Superior Court to resolve custody, support and property issues or to terminate their relationships if they do not qualify under the summary termination laws.

---

[1] *Marvin* v. *Marvin* (1976) 18 Cal.3d 550. This case was a lawsuit by Michelle Triola Marvin, the live-in girlfriend of actor Lee Marvin, who claimed that Lee Marvin had made various promises to her about the property and income acquired during their relationship. Some people refer to this as a *palimony* action.

Dissolution will permanently terminate the domestic partnership, divide property, order spousal support if appropriate, determine child custody and child support if there are children from the relationship and return the partners to the status of single persons. Legal separation, though available, is unlikely to be used often. Legal separation resolves all property, support and custody issues, and the parties are declared separated, which shields each from liability for the other's debts and means all earned income and property which either acquires will be separate property, but the domestic partnership is not terminated and neither partner can enter a new domestic partnership or marry. The most typical reasons opposite-sex couples have used legal separation rather than dissolution have been because one or both feel a strong prohibition, usually religious in origin, against dissolution or, because, by retaining the legal tie between them, they can continue to provide health benefits for the other. One further disadvantage in electing a legal separation is the practical aspect that if the parties want a dissolution after the legal separation has been granted, they will have to re-file for dissolution and wait for another six-month period for the dissolution to be finalized, although all the property, support and custody issues will have been resolved.

There are two bases for dissolution and legal separation in California: *irreconcilable differences* and *incurable insanity*. The term *irreconcilable differences* means there has been an "irremediable breakdown" of the relationship to the extent that no further efforts can salvage the marriage.[2] If one partner declares there are irreconcilable differences, the other partner cannot compel counseling or any other intervention to try to save the relationship. Irreconcilable differences do not need to be proven. Many clients want to use *incurable insanity* to describe their soon-to-be former spouse or partner, but conditions justifying these grounds are extremely rare. The partner seeking to terminate the relationship must prove by medical or psychiatric testimony that

---

[2] California Family Code section 2310.

the other partner suffers from some severe mental health problem that is unlikely to be resolved, that is, that the partner is incurably insane. Typically the mentally disturbed spouse or partner would have to be institutionalized. A nullity, more commonly referred to as an annulment, perpetrates a strange legal fiction: it treats the marriage as having never happened, but the court will still handle property, support and custody issues. A nullity is a legal process. A religious annulment is spiritual and does not affect the legal status. A legal nullity may not satisfy the requirements for a religious annulment. The legal grounds for nullity are more numerous, though each is narrowly restricted and must be proven by the party who seeks the nullity. The court either determines that the marriage was void from the beginning, for example, because of bigamy or incest,[3] or the court considers the marriage voidable[4] because of the status of one or both of the parties at the time of the marriage.

Residency Requirements

Typically the party who petitions for dissolution, nullity or legal separation must have been a resident of the state for six

---

[3] Grounds for declaring marriages void:

Incest: the spouses are close blood relatives.
Bigamy: a spouse was knowingly married to another living person at the time of marriage.

[4] Grounds for declaring marriages voidable:

Underage: a spouse was below age 18 years at the time of marriage and did not obtain parental consent or a court order permitting the marriage.
Prior existing marriage: a spouse married on the mistaken belief that his or her previous marriage had ended in the death of the other spouse, who in fact was still living.
Unsound mind: a spouse could not and has not formed the intent to marry due to a mental condition.
Fraud: deception regarding a significant matter that led to the marriage and continued until the breakup.
Force: threats or acts of harm were used to force one spouse into the marriage.
Incapacity: a spouse was and continues to be physically unable to consummate the marriage.

months and a resident of the county in which the dissolution is filed for at least three months for the court to be able to have the authority to hear and decide the case. Family Code section 299(d) says that a dissolution, nullity or legal separation shall follow the same procedures as those relating to marriage. There is, however, an exception. Because the parties consent to the jurisdiction of the California superior courts in registering as domestic partners, proceedings may be filed in the superior courts "...even if neither domestic partner is a resident of, or maintains a domicile in, the state at the time the proceedings are filed."[5] This is a logical difference since the California domestic partnerships are not necessarily recognized outside of the state. If an opposite-sex couple married in California and moved to Michigan, for example, he and she could later obtain a divorce in Michigan if their marriage ended. By contrast, a same-sex couple who registered in California as domestic partners and moved to Michigan might have no legal means to end their relationship there. They cannot ignore their domestic partnership and pretend it does not exist. Since they might not be able to terminate the domestic partnership in their new state of residence, AB 205 allows them to use the California court system for that purpose even if they do not reside in California any longer.

Need for Additional Legal Action

Superior Courts can resolve property issues in the dissolution of a marriage or partnership. However, no authority exists for the Superior Court to deal with the pre-registration assets of the partners in a family law case, even if the partners have lived together for a number of years. Consequently, the partners may have to file a second action, this one a civil lawsuit, to divide the pre-registration property. This civil lawsuit complicates the situation because, unlike a family law matter which is heard and decided only by a judge, civil suits may entitle one to a jury. In family law cases, attorney fees may be awarded,

---

[5] California Family Code section 299(d).

though that is not the case in civil suits such as these.

Property Division

In a dissolution, legal separation or nullity action, the court will order a division of the community assets. The goal of the court is to make an equal division of the property. Equal division does not mean that if a couple has an eight-place setting of china, each will receive four place settings. Instead, the process is approached using a balance sheet model: the property and debts awarded to each spouse should come close to being of equal value. Naturally there are numerous exceptions. For example, one parent may be awarded the use of the family home if there are children of school age.

While it seems as though property should be the easy part of a family law action because it is about things, there are many legal concepts that come into the equation. This is the point at which it becomes necessary to characterize the property as community, separate or pre-registration. Contributions from separate property must be considered to determine if either partner is entitled to any reimbursements.[6] The value of the property is also significant, and different rules apply about the date at which property is to be valued, that is, at the date of separation or at a date just before any trial, if a trial is necessary.

Unfortunately, some people hide assets or misrepresent the property's value to their partner. In the case of businesses, the couple may have used the assets casually, buying an occasional roll of stamps through the business for use at home, driving the company car for weekend pleasure trips or writing off various personal expenses as business expenses. In the light of day before a judge, people sometimes do not want to admit to such casual and perhaps taxable conduct. Likewise, when one person

---

[6] Effective January 1, 2005, under law enacted by SB 1407 (Kuehl), California Family Code section 2640 will require reimbursement when one partner uses his or her separate property to help the other partner acquire separate property, unless there has been a written transmutation of the property or a written waiver of this right to reimbursement.

runs the business, that partner may have ways to make his or her income appear less for purposes of child or spousal support determinations. A court has the authority to award offsetting amounts for any intentional impairment of a spouse's interest in community property, including awards equal to 100% of the value of the property at its highest value plus attorney fees and costs.[7] Such conduct violates the fiduciary duty each partner owes the other to protect and maximize the property of the partners.

Retirement Plans

This category of property deserves mention because so many retirement plans either are federally-funded, federally-regulated and because the division of retirement plans can create federal tax liability. For most retirement plans for married couples, a family law court can order the plan divided in whatever appropriate share with no tax consequence to either spouse. Typically when one takes funds prior to the payout of the retirement benefit, that is considered a withdrawal and may be taxable and subject to penalties for early withdrawal. Giving a spouse part of one's retirement funds is considered a withdrawal, but the Internal Revenue Code provides an exception for such a transfer and does not consider it taxable, and no penalties are imposed. The tax exception is unavailable for domestic partners because it is a federal benefit not affected by AB 205, and a court-ordered distribution or division of one's retirement would be taxable and subject to penalty. Separate from the issue of whether the transfer of retirement funds will be considered an early withdrawal and subject to income tax and penalties is the issue that has come up repeatedly about the impact of AB 205: will the transfer of these benefits also constitute a transfer of separate property to the recipient partner and thus become a taxable gift?

The effect of AB 205 for plans governed by the Employee Retirement Income Security Act of 1974 (ERISA) probably will

---

[7] California Family Code sections 1101, 2602.

require litigation to resolve. ERISA generally preempts state laws relating to community property to the extent those laws affect either the administration of the covered plan or the benefits the plan must provide. If courts hold that AB 205 is preempted by ERISA, then covered plans will not have to recognize family law court orders for domestic partners.[8]

Spousal Support

Spousal support can be either temporary or permanent. The duration of the relationship is probably the most significant factor in determining the length of the support obligation. For domestic partners, this again raises the issue of the beginning date of the relationship. Under AB 2580, the date of registration should set the starting point in calculating the length of the relationship. In addition, the court will consider the age and the health of the partners, the earning ability of each partner and their expenses, whether there are minor children in the home and also will consider the style of living that the partners have experienced. The court will also consider whether one partner helped the other obtain an education, training, a career or a professional license, whether either partner stayed home to care for the minor children and whether there was domestic violence in the relationship. The tax impact of the support is another factor the court reviews.[9]

The courts have authority to award spousal support to domestic partners. For married spouses, spousal support is considered income to the recipient and is tax-deductible for the payor.[10] However, California law requires the court to consider

---

[8] There are finely prescribed orders necessary to direct the division of retirement plans and payment to the non-covered spouse in family law actions. The orders are referred to as Qualified Domestic Relations Orders or QDROs (pronounced **quad**′ ro).

[9] California Family Code section 4320.

[10] Although this may sound unfair to make spousal support taxable, if one realizes that the payor is actually transferring income on which he or she would have to pay taxes, it is clear that the payor is just passing the income through to the recipient who then bears the burden of taxes on this income.

the "immediate and specific tax consequences..." in awards made in a dissolution, legal separation or nullity action.[11] As a result, the courts are going to have to consider the fact that the payor spouse has no tax deductibility available and has to bear the tax consequences on the support paid.

The court can order spousal support payable by a wage assignment served on the payor partner's employer. The employer is then obligated to deduct the support due and pay it directly to the recipient partner from the payor partner's paycheck. If an employer is not aware that an employee is gay, receipt of a wage assignment order for support payable to someone of the same gender will no doubt *out* the employee partner to the employer.

> Garry and Jorge were domestic partners for seven years before they filed for dissolution. They have two children from their relationship. Jorge has a net monthly income, after proper withholding, of $4000 per month. He pays $1000 per month for the support of the children. Garry has a net income of $2000 per month.

The law in this case would award temporary support to Garry during the pendency of the dissolution proceeding, that is, from the time he petitions the court for temporary support until a final judgment is entered. Many courts use a formula for setting the amount for temporary support. The goal at this point in the proceedings is to try to maintain the living circumstances as close as possible to the way they were before the couple's separation. Practically, this is usually impossible since the same income now must be used to finance two residences while continuing to pay any community bills. In this example, using the Santa Clara County guidelines, which are used by a number of counties, the court would reduce Jorge's income by the amount of child support he pays. His net income would then be $3000. 40% of that

[11] California Family Code section 4320(j).

amount, $1200, would be available for spousal support. However, the amount would be offset by half of Garry's net income which, in this case, would be $1000. Garry would get $200 per month temporary support. Obviously the amount of Garry's income can substantially influence the amount of temporary support received. If, by the agreement of the partners, Garry had always stayed home, especially if it had been for the purpose of caring for their children, Garry probably would receive the full $1200. If there is any indication that one partner is deliberately not working or has deliberately quit a job to force the other partner to pay support, the court can impute the ability to earn a certain base amount to a partner. The imputation of earning ability more typically is a factor in the award of permanent support.

A permanent support order is always based on the court's weighing of the factors mentioned above. The term *permanent* is a misnomer: the support may be permanent in long-term partnerships or in some other special circumstances, but in most instances support does not continue indefinitely. A rule of thumb, and it is only that because there are so many variables, is that permanent support will last about half the duration of the partnership or marriage. Permanent support also is not permanent because it ends upon remarriage of the recipient partner or the death of either partner. Rarely, too, is the amount of the support permanent because in most instances it can be modified by either party based on a significant change in circumstances. The parties are entitled to make annual demands on each other for information about their respective incomes to see if a modification of support is due.

One question that may have to be decided is what effect a subsequent domestic partnership will have on the obligation to pay support. For married couples, if a court has awarded spousal support to one spouse and that spouse subsequently remarries, spousal support ends. If the law under AB 205 is to apply in the same manner to domestic partners as it would to spouses, then one should expect that entering into a new registered domestic partnership should be the equivalent of remarriage and will terminate prior spousal support obligations.

The issue of spousal support is much more complex than these few paragraphs would imply. The longer the duration of the partnership, the greater the likelihood that support will be awarded to the lower income partner. Partners can waive spousal support even in a court proceeding, but courts are hesitant to allow a waiver because once it is made, it is irrevocable. The court will make considerable effort to determine that the partner waiving support has done so knowingly and voluntarily.

Child Custody

There are two aspects to custody: physical custody, which determines with whom the child resides, and legal custody, which gives a parent the right to make decisions about the health, safety, welfare and education of his or her child. When a couple is together, each partner has an equal right to the control and custody of the child, and each has an equal responsibility for the child's welfare and support.

Legal and physical custody become important if the partners dissolve their relationship. At that time, if they cannot agree on a plan for custody of the child, a court will make the determination about who has physical custody, whether the physical custody is with one partner only or shared, and whether the parties will share joint legal custody. The issue of physical custody, if not agreed upon by the partners, will be based on a judge's determination of what living arrangement will be in the best interest of the child or children.

In its most simplified version, child custody depends on one thing: the best interest of the child. Customarily, the court struggles conscientiously in trying to decide what is best. This is often further complicated by the fact that the parents are hurt or angry about the end of their relationship, and, in their anger and pain, they often cannot concede that the other parent has anything worthwhile to offer their children. In such situations, it is the children who lose, and it is the attorneys who *win* as their fees mount. Custody can also become an unfortunately ill-conceived bargaining point in property or other disputes between the parents.[12]

There are several other factors that a court will consider in the process. A court will give weight in awarding custody to the parent who is most likely to allow the other parent regular and frequent contact with the child. Additionally, a court likes to maintain the *status quo* for a child, that is, the preference is to keep the child in the same school, near the same friends and generally to maintain life as close to the way it was before the parents decided to end their relationship. The court will also consider the wishes of the child if the child is of sufficient age "... to form an intelligent preference."[13] There is no age at which a child gets to choose with whom he or she will live; the court will always decide what is in the best interest of the child.[14]

The best possible outcome is for the parents to agree to

---

[12] I had a colleague, a professional, who was going through a divorce. He had a young child, but he had little, if any, contact on a daily or even weekly basis with his daughter. He was caught up in his work, and he had little interest in his child. When it came time for the couple to discuss the division of community property, the man had no interest in giving his wife any of the value in his professional practice. He concocted a strategy: he directed his attorney to seek joint or primary custody of his daughter with the goal that he would offer to give up his custody request if his wife would give up her claim for half the value of his practice.

[13] California Family Code section 3042.

[14] I once represented a mother who had custody of her 17-year-old son, although he was staying with his father and refused to come home. His father, who was unemployed due to some mental health issues, wanted the boy to stay with him and petitioned the court to award him custody. The young man had been an excellent student but had started cutting school and failing his classes since he went to his father's house. After a trial, the court confirmed custody to the mother and ordered the boy to go home. I got a note from his mother many years later saying her son had made up his academic deficiencies, gone on to college, graduated and was working in a high-paying and satisfying job. The judge decided it would be in the best interest of this 17-year-old child to be with a parent who would provide supervision and get him through high school.

a custodial plan. If they cannot, the court will refer them to family mediation before it will make any long-term decisions. Usually the court will make a temporary order while the family goes to mediation and then will make an order after receiving a mediator's report. If the parents still do not agree with the mediator's recommendations, there will be a trial before final orders are made. However, in one sense there are never any final orders because either parent can ask the court to revisit the matter of custody as the needs of the child change over time and the circumstances of the parents change as well.

Child Visitation

A number of years ago, once the court had decided which parent would have custody, a visitation schedule was worked out for the non-custodial parent. Visitation is still awarded to parents, but more and more often parents work out a joint custodial arrangement. In many ways a custodial arrangement is preferable because it creates a greater sense of commitment when one has custody of his or her child rather than just the right to visit. Any visitation order is also based on the best interest of the child, and a court will award visitation to a parent unless such visits are detrimental to the child. Additionally, the court has the authority to allow reasonable visitation to "any other person having an interest in the welfare of the child."[15] Visitation can also be granted to a stepparent[16] or to a grandparent.[17]

Child Support

Twenty-five years ago, California had spiral-ring binders that contained tables that dictated child support dollar amounts. One looked for the correct page indicating how many children the couple had and then looked down one column to see the

---

[15] California Family Code section 3100.

[16] California Family Code section 3101.

[17] California Family Code section 3103.

husband's salary and across the top row to find the wife's salary. The point at which they intersected was the amount the higher income-earning spouse paid to the lower income-earning spouse. Today the formula is so complex that, in practice, it requires a special computer software program and requires greater detail about the amounts withheld from a parent's income, including the rules that dictate the proper tax withholding, and specific information about the number of days, holidays and vacation periods a child or children are with each parent.[18]

Child support is a right that belongs to the child, and no parent can waive support from the other parent. The guideline amounts are presumed to be appropriate, though parents can agree to a lesser amount if they can show that they know what the guideline amounts should be, there has been no coercion to take a lesser amount and the needs of the children will be adequately met.[19] Child support can also include additional expenses beyond the guideline amounts, for example, for child care or special medical or educational needs of a child. One cannot force another parent to pay for private school for a child, but if the child had been in private school for some time and the parties had intended that kind of education to continue, the court can factor those expenses into a child support order.

The principles that a court must follow in awarding child support also define the philosophy underlying California laws about the need to support children:

> (a) A parent's first and principal obligation is to support his or her minor children according to the parent's circumstances and station in life.
> (b) Both parents are mutually responsible for the support of their children.
> (c) The guideline takes into account each parent's actual income and level of responsibility for the children.
> (d) Each parent should pay for the support of the

---

[18] The actual formula is defined in California Family Code section 4055. It is set out in full in Appendix H.

[19] California Family Code section 4065.

> children according to his or her ability.
> (e) The guideline seeks to place the interests of children as the state's top priority.
> (f) Children should share in the standard of living of both parents. Child support may therefore appropriately improve the standard of living of the custodial household to improve the lives of the children.
> (g) Child support orders in cases in which both parents have high levels of responsibility for the children should reflect the increased costs of raising the children in two homes and should minimize significant disparities in the children's living standards in the two homes.
> (h) The financial needs of the children should be met through private financial resources as much as possible.
> (i) It is presumed that a parent having primary physical responsibility for the children contributes a significant portion of available resources for the support of the children.
> (j) The guideline seeks to encourage fair and efficient settlements of conflicts between parents and seeks to minimize the need for litigation.
> (k) The guideline is intended to be presumptively correct in all cases, and only under special circumstances should child support orders fall below the child support mandated by the guideline formula.
> (l) Child support orders must ensure that children actually receive fair, timely, and sufficient support reflecting the state's high standard of living and high costs of raising children compared to other states.[20]

While most people would agree, in theory, with these principles, too often couples find child support and child custody issues to be more related to how they feel about each other and how angry they are than to what may be best for their children. Parents who have not been the primary caregiver for the children may decide they want primary custody because they know so much of the child support formula relies on the amount of time the children spend with each parent.

---

[20] California Family Code section 4053.

Child support obligations continue until a child is 18 years old and has graduated from high school, but not beyond age 19. Support can be ordered for a child who is an adult, but only if the child is incapacitated from earning a living and is without sufficient means.[21] This support obligation is intended to be the equal responsibility of both parents.

Child support is payable by wage assignment, as are spousal support obligations. The payment of child support is expected to take priority over all other financial obligations, including debts to creditors.[22] Failure to pay court-ordered child support can result in money being taken from the payor parent's state tax refunds, and being in arrears on child support means that many state licensing boards will not renew the payor parent's professional license. The custodial parent can also file a civil lawsuit against the non-paying parent for unpaid support.[23] Failure to pay support can also be addressed by a contempt citation in which the court orders the individual to provide a valid factual and legal reason for the failure to pay support; short of being run over by a tractor-trailer, few excuses are acceptable. One can be subject to five days in jail and a fine for each violation of an order. If the non-custodial parent fails to pay and, in doing so, forces the custodial parent and child to receive social welfare payments, the District Attorney in the county where the child resides will seek reimbursement from the non-paying parent for the support paid on behalf of the child.

There is a silver lining to child support obligations: the law requires an adult child to support his or her parent, to the extent the adult child is able to do so, if the parent is unable to maintain himself or herself by work.[24]

---

[21] California Family Code section 3910.

[22] California Family Code section 4011.

[23] California Family Code section 4000.

[24] California Family Code section 4400.

Six-Month Waiting Period

There is a minimal six-month waiting period between the time one files a petition and the date on which the court can end the relationship or declare the parties legally separated. Even if the couple is amenable to ending their domestic partnership and has all their requisite paperwork filed shortly after initiating the process, the status of the relationship cannot be changed until at least six months have passed. During this period, neither partner is legally able to enter into another registered domestic partnership or into a marriage.[25]

---

[25] One is always legally able to marry his or her domestic partner without first terminating the domestic partnership should marriage ever become a reality for gay couples.

Chapter 13

Domestic Partnerships and Criminal Law

Though we may think primarily of property rights, child custody and support when discussing domestic partnerships, since they are a substitute for the right to marry, the implications of AB 205 are also found in the area of criminal law. Because marital status is a factor in the applicability of various criminal laws, these areas need to be addressed as well.

Spousal Privilege

When a person becomes involved in the legal system, it is not always by choice. For example, someone might be the victim of a crime, a witness to an event or a party to a lawsuit. Sometimes an individual files a lawsuit and initiates the legal action. However, simply because a person is in the legal system, there is no reason that his entire life should be suddenly open to scrutiny, especially if the individual has been brought into the process involuntarily. For example, a spouse who saw a counselor for personal issues does not want to be forced to reveal everything about the therapy because her spouse files for dissolution of the marriage and for custody of their children.

One of the basic concepts in law is the concept of *privilege*. Privilege is the right to maintain confidentiality in a court proceeding about a communication that was confidential originally. The persons with whom one can expect a confidential communication are limited to special relationships in which the other person stands in a particular position of authority or trust.

When an individual goes to the doctor, the communications with the doctor are confidential, and the doctor is obligated to maintain the patient's confidentiality. The same is true when an individual goes to a psychotherapist or to a clergyperson or to an attorney.

In the most basic terms, privilege allows a person to refuse to testify, and to prevent another from testifying, about the contents of a confidential communication. Privilege is not absolute, and there are times when otherwise confidential information can or must be admitted in court. One relationship to which the concept of privilege applies is to the relationship between husband and wife and now, as of January 1, 2005, to the relationship between registered domestic partners. Again, because AB 205 is a state law, this privilege will only apply in state courts.

California has two versions of privilege when it comes to spouses[1]: a spouse can refuse to testify against his or her spouse in a legal proceeding,[2] and a spouse can prevent the other spouse from testifying against him or her about matters the spouse conveyed, orally or in writing, in confidence to the other.[3]

In the first instance, if a spouse is subpoenaed to testify against his or her spouse, the subpoenaed spouse can refuse to testify. This choice is in the discretion of the testifying spouse who also has the ability to agree to testify. As with many protections under the law, there are numerous exceptions, such as when there is litigation between the two spouses, including family law matters, conservatorship proceedings and competency hearings, and in cases involving various crimes committed against the other partner and against certain family members.

---

[1] See Appendix D for the full text of these laws and the related provisions and exceptions.

[2] Evidence Code section 970.

[3] Evidence Code section 980.

> Michelle and Scarlett are registered domestic partners. Scarlett is in the middle of a civil lawsuit brought by her former business partner to obtain an accounting of the business's assets. The former co-owner suspects Scarlett took home various property of the business and failed to account for them when the business folded. The former co-owner now subpoenas Michelle to get her to reveal what property is kept at their home and whether the property is something Scarlett brought home from the business.

The law in this case means that Michelle, as Scarlett's registered domestic partner, has the right, the *privilege*, to refuse to testify in the lawsuit. However, if Michelle agrees to allow Scarlett to call her as a witness, if Michelle answers questions from Scarlett's attorney, she must answer questions from the former co-owner's attorney.

The second version of privilege deals with confidential communications. During marriage, one spouse may confide something to the other spouse which is clearly intended to be, and to remain, confidential. In such an instance, the spouse who made the confidential communication can prevent the other spouse from testifying. There are several restrictions: the communication must be made during the marriage; it does not extend to physical facts which are observed by the testifying spouse; and there are exceptions, such as situations in which one spouse commits a crime against the other spouse.

Clark and Jimmy are registered domestic partners. Clark comes home one night and tells Jimmy that he really needs to talk and unburden himself. He tells Jimmy of a night several years ago when he was working a night shift at a convenience store. It was shortly after the two of them met and got together. He desperately needed $300 more for school tuition. A customer came into the store and flashed a big wad of money when he made a purchase. Clark recognized the man as someone who worked at a nearby store. The man came in regularly on Friday nights and always had a great deal of cash. Clark assumed that Fridays were the man's payday. One Friday, Clark called in sick and waited in the dark behind the store for the man to come in. The man entered the store, made his purchase and walked out the door, still putting his cash back into his wallet. Clark, wearing a hooded sweatshirt, dashed out, knocked the man to the ground, took his wallet and ran home. There was almost $800 in the wallet, and Clark kept it all. He tells Jimmy that he saw the man earlier today at a gas station, and that he felt terrible about stealing the money. A few days later, police come to talk to Clark after the man reports to them that he saw Clark, who he thought was the man who mugged him. The case comes up for trial, and the District Attorney subpoenas Jimmy as a witness against Clark.

The law in this case would allow Clark to claim spousal privilege and prevent Jimmy from testifying if they have registered as domestic partners prior to the conversation in which Clark confided his criminal conduct. If the conversation was before the couple registered, Clark will not be able to prevent Jimmy from testifying about what he revealed. Under AB 205, spousal privilege now applies to registered domestic partners. However, the parties must be able to prove they are properly registered. Also, the use of privilege is all-or-nothing: once a person starts testifying against his or her spouse, one must answer all questions and cannot pick and choose which he will answer and which he will not.

Crime Victim Leave

On January 1, 2004, a law went into effect that allows employees who are victims of crime, and employees who are *closely related* to a crime victim, to take time off from work to attend related court and legal proceedings.[4] Employers cannot fire, retaliate or discriminate against employees who ask for or take this leave. Violations of the law can create a vulnerability to misdemeanor penalties for the employer. There is no time limit on the amount of leave nor is there a requirement of any minimum notice by an employee of the need to take this time off. It is reasonable to characterize a domestic partner as *closely related* as of January 1, 2005.

Right to Use Force to Protect One's Spouse

California law states: "Any necessary force may be used to protect from wrongful injury the person or property of oneself, or of a wife, husband, child, parent, or other relative, or member of one's family, or of a ward, servant, master, or guest."[5] Defending one's same-sex partner previously was not acceptable. Under the new law, one partner can protect the other domestic partner and the couple's children. The justifiable homicide exception is also applicable. Justifiable homicide requires more than fear for one's life or the life of a spouse or child: there must be circumstances, conditions or behaviors that would lead an individual to believe that there is imminent danger of great bodily harm.[6]

---

[4] California Labor Code section 230.2.

[5] California Civil Code section 50.

[6] California Penal Code section 197.

Marsha and Roberta are registered domestic partners. About 3:00 one morning, there is a loud pounding at their front door. Marsha goes to see what's going on. Roberta hears loud voices, crashing sounds and Marsha screaming. Roberta grabs a pistol she keeps locked in their closet and goes to check on Marsha. When she enters the living room, there are two men yelling at Marsha to give them her car keys.

The intruders see Roberta and one grabs Marsha and draws a large knife from a sheath on his belt, raising his arm as though he is about to stab Marsha. Roberta fires her gun at the man, and he is hit and falls to the floor. The other man flees, and the women call 9-1-1. The wounded man dies en route to the hospital.

The law in this case would consider Roberta's actions to be justifiable homicide in the defense of her domestic partner. There were circumstances and behaviors that led Roberta to reasonably believe that Marsha was about to be seriously harmed or killed. The men forced their way into the residence in the middle of the night and, when confronted, the one man drew a knife and raised his arm in a way to suggest that he was about to stab Marsha. Roberta will not be charged.

The initial situation is the same: about 3:00 one morning, there is a loud pounding at their front door. Marsha goes to see what's going on. Roberta hears loud voices, crashing sounds and Marsha screaming. Roberta grabs a pistol she keeps locked in their closet and goes to check on Marsha. When she enters the living room, there are two men yelling at Marsha to give them her car keys.

The intruders see Roberta and one grabs Marsha by the arms, shakes her and warns menacingly, "You'll pay for this." He has no weapon, and other than grabbing Marsha, he does nothing to harm her physically or to otherwise threaten her. Roberta shoots the man, who later dies.

The law in this case will likely result in criminal charges against Roberta because the force she used was excessive in relation to the circumstances since there was no indication the man would cause great bodily harm. She was free to use force to protect Marsha, her domestic partner, but one always is required to use force equal to the situation. Deadly force requires a realistic fear that one is about to be seriously harmed or killed.

Domestic Violence

The definition of domestic violence as presently written includes violence occurring between co-habitants. Co-habitation was determined by whether the couple described themselves to others as being husband and wife, whether the two engaged in sexual relations, and whether they shared a residence, income and expenses or property. There no longer will be any need to question whether there is a dating or engagement relationship or inquire into the intimacies of one's relationship to determine whether domestic violence has occurred. Domestic violence now includes abuse against any adult who is a registered domestic partner.[7] Laws allowing leave from work for victims of domestic violence who need to take time to handle legal, medical, psychological and other safety concerns also apply to domestic partners and their children.[8]

Domestic violence is an unfortunate reality for some same-sex couples as it is for some opposite-sex couples. No one knows what the incidence of domestic violence is in the gay community. Most who witness it or hear of it feel that it is serious and needs intervention. One of the challenges is finding resources and treatment programs for these couples. A man battered by his male partner typically will have no shelter or safe house available where he can take refuge. Because there are so few resources designed specifically for gay couples, to enter treatment

---

[7] Violence against a child is child abuse, and the relationship of the adult is not relevant to whether the violence is seen as abuse.

[8] California Labor Code section2 230, 230.1.

programs, couples must be prepared, during this vulnerable time, to come out.

> Unfortunately the pattern for Billy and Jim was the same as that for many couples in which there is domestic abuse: things go along well for awhile and then Jim starts getting angry and nothing Billy does is right. Finally, the tension escalates until Jim hits Billy and shoves him down. The next day, Jim is apologetic, promises that he'll never be physically aggressive again and takes Billy out to a delightful dinner and to hear a jazz singer at a nearby hotel. All is well until tonight when the tension boils over. This time Jim cannot stop himself, and he batters Billy seriously. Billy pushes Jim to the ground, runs out of the apartment and goes to a neighbor's house to call the police. The police respond and try to sort things out to determine who is responsible for what.

The law in this case should view this as domestic violence. If these two people were an opposite-sex couple, law enforcement would not hesitate to approach this as a case of domestic violence. Because it is two men, the officers could easily presume they are "mutual combatants" and assess whether either or both had committed a crime. Rather than recognizing the situation as being a highly volatile domestic violence situation, the officers might not use interventions or provide referrals for programs related to domestic violence.

Incarcerated Partners

Prisoners in California, not in federal facilities, may, in some situations, be allowed overnight visitation with immediate family members. Immediate family members are those persons related by blood, marriage or adoption. Additionally, the Penal Code allows inmates the right to marry.[9] Presumably a prisoner and his or her domestic partner will be allowed to register and to enjoy all the rights of spouses as they apply to an incarcerated

[9] California Penal Code section 2601(e).

partner, although this would only apply to state prisons. Because of the stigma and related risks still associated with same-sex relationships, this may not be an option a prisoner might elect, but the right exists nonetheless.

Spouses of Public Officials

It is a misdemeanor in California to reveal that someone is a law enforcement officer or the spouse or child of a law enforcement officer and to disclose the residence address or phone number of the individuals if the disclosure is done maliciously and to obstruct justice, that is, to attempt to threaten or intimidate the law enforcement officer. If physical harm comes to the spouse or child, the crime becomes a felony.[10] It is also unlawful to threaten to kill or seriously harm any elected public official, county public defender, county clerk, exempt appointee of the governor, judge, or Deputy Commissioner of the Board of Prison Terms, or their staff or immediate families.[11] This applies if the individual has a domestic partner. An assault against many governmental officials, judges, jurors *or* the immediate family of these individuals, in retaliation for or to prevent the performance of the victim's duties is a crime.[12] This applies to one's domestic partner and children.

Filing a False Declaration of Domestic Partnership

The domestic partnership law has its own built-in criminal component: filing an intentionally and materially false Declaration

---

[10] California Penal Code section 146e.

[11] California Penal Code section 76.

[12] California Penal Code section 217.1. This includes specifically the President, Vice President, any Governor, any judicial officer (local, state, or federal), any official of the United States, or any state or territory holding elective office, any mayor or city council member, county supervisor, sheriff, district attorney, any prosecutor or assistant prosecutor, any peace officer, or any juror.

of Domestic Partnership shall be punishable as a misdemeanor.[13] Such a provision makes sense since a domestic partnership confers certain rights that would not otherwise exist for two individuals. While opposite-sex couples obtain rights from marriage, marriage still requires a more involved process of obtaining a license, having a ceremony, either civil or religious, and filing the license. The process of becoming domestic partners is a simplified one of filling out a form, having signatures notarized and mailing it in. Because the process is so simplified and requires only a notary, who may not even know the two individuals personally, the ability to file a false declaration for purposes of obtaining benefits is substantial. A notary's acknowledgment only attests that the individual appeared before the notary and provided sufficient evidence to verify that he or she was the person who actually signed the document. The notary does not attest to the truthfulness of the declarations of the individuals signing the form.

---

[13] California Family Code section 298(c).

Chapter 14

Some Last Thoughts About New Beginnings

Like a long lonely stream
I keep runnin' towards a dream
Movin' on, movin' on
Like a branch on a tree
I keep reachin' to be free
Movin' on, movin' on.

'Cause there's a place in the sun
Where there's hope for ev'ryone
Where my poor restless heart's gotta run.
There's a place in the sun
And before my life is done
Got to find me a place in the sun.
–Stevie Wonder

Just as AB 205 is the beginning of countless changes socially, legally and personally, so, too, is this book just a beginning. Each day seems to bring another idea or nuance about the implications of this law. Typical of any laws, as well-written as they may be and as carefully crafted as the authors think they are, it is often not until the laws encounter real-life situations that their full impact is realized or their shortcomings materialize. Domestic partnerships in California are a work-in-progress. Superimposed on the practicalities of implementing these laws are the evolving politics of our times. Will there be further legal and political challenges to AB 205? Will the attempt to amend the United States Constitution be revived, and what will the implications of such federal politics be? In the November 2004 elections, voters in eleven states approved laws limiting provision of equal rights to gays and lesbians within those states. Will the climate in those states impact the rights of citizens in California? At the start of the new legislative session on December 6, 2004, one bill was introduced that would define marriage as a civil contract between two people, not a man and a woman, and two proposed constitutional amendments were introduced to prohibit gay marriage. On December 21, 2004, a California Appellate Court denied an attempt to prevent the implementation of AB 205 on January 1, 2005.

With the political climate fluid and strangely conflicted, the other question that is important is whether domestic partners will be willing to take the personal risks to *come out* in the ways necessary to claim their rights under AB 205 and under similar state statutes across the country. To those readers who are not gay, it is difficult to convey the significance of this factor in determining how AB 205 will unfold in real life. Also, for the non-gay reader, there will be the challenge of anticipating problems for domestic partners and stretching beyond comfort levels by making gentle inquiries when they are needed.

AB 205 itself states that the new law "... shall be construed liberally in order to secure to eligible couples who register as domestic partners the full range of legal rights, protections and benefits, as well as all of the responsibilities, obligations, and duties to each other, to their children, to third parties and to the state, as the laws of California extend to and impose upon spouses."[1] The legislative intent is encouraging, but it is impossible to predict what this directive will mean in practical terms. There will undoubtedly be a number of court challenges. However, it is clear that so much of the success of California's efforts to secure legal rights and responsibilities for domestic partners will depend upon changes at the federal level.

This book, like AB 205, is the beginning. A simple search of an online legal research service garnered 2368 *hits* for the words *spouse, spouses,* and *spousal*, 2257 hits for *husband*, 2394

---

[1] AB 205, Section 15.

hits for *wife* and 1899 hits for *marriage.* There are obviously hundreds of other applications of AB 205 and interpretations of its effects that will be made in the coming years. There are rights to remain in rent-controlled property, to be exempted from certain property tax reappraisal events, to use senior housing and student housing as domestic partners, to have state government hiring preferences as the surviving domestic partners of veterans and of disabled veterans and to receive public employment retirement plans and survivor benefits equivalent to those provided to spouses. The list continues.

The challenge for the professionals and business people is to expand their creativity when it comes to any instance in which the marital status of a client or customer is relevant.[2] The challenge for courts is to be deliberate in making decisions, recognizing that what is good for an opposite-sex couple may not be good for a same-sex couple. The challenge for gay and lesbian couples will be to educate themselves about the realities of domestic partnership, make informed choices and commit to doing what they must do to claim their rights and meet their responsibilities.

---

[2] One of my favorite people is Bob Hawke, a sales person at Elm Ford in Woodland, California. Bob is the kind of man that you want to stop by and have a cup of coffee with, and he can talk with you about anything from Biblical antiquities to baseball. At my invitation, he attended a speech I gave on the implications of AB 205. Afterwards he told me that he had never realized how hard coming out must be for some people and that he needed to go back and educate his colleagues because starting January 1, 2005, there could be credit and title issues for gay clients that he had not considered and that he was sure others had not either. It was important to him not only that he did not offend anyone, but also that he did not ignore their rights and their options. That attitude is considerate, and it's good business, too.

APPENDIX A

THE CALIFORNIA DOMESTIC PARTNER RIGHTS AND RESPONSIBILITIES ACT OF 2003

Assembly Bill No. 205
CHAPTER 421

Introduced by Assembly Members Goldberg, Kehoe, Koretz, Laird, and Leno
(Principal Coauthor: Assembly Member Wesson)
(Coauthors: Assembly Members Berg, Bermudez, Chan, Chu, Diaz, Dymally, Firebaugh, Frommer, Hancock, Levine, Lieber, Longville, Lowenthal, Montanez, Nation, Nunez, Oropeza, Pavley, Simitian, Steinberg, Vargas, and Yee)
(Coauthors: Senators Burton, Cedillo, Romero, and Vasconcellos)

An act to amend Sections 297, 298, and 298.5 of, to add Sections 297.5, 299.2, and 299.3 to, to repeal Section 299.5 of, and to repeal and add Section 299 of, the Family Code, to amend Section 14771 of the Government Code, and to amend Section 3 of Chapter 447 of the Statutes of 2002, relating to domestic partnerships.
[Approved by Governor September 19, 2003. Filed with Secretary of State September 22, 2003.]

LEGISLATIVE COUNSEL'S DIGEST
AB 205, Goldberg. Domestic partners.

Existing law provides for the issuance of a marriage license and specifies the rights and obligations of married persons. Existing law also provides for the establishment and the termination of domestic partnerships. Existing law requires the Secretary of State to prepare and distribute forms for creating and terminating domestic partnerships. Existing law specifies the requirements for completing the form necessary to create a domestic partnership and provides that a violation of this provision is a misdemeanor. This bill would enact the California Domestic Partner

Rights and Responsibilities Act of 2003. The bill would modify the procedure and the accompanying form for terminating domestic partnerships, and require additional duties of the Secretary of State in relation, as specified. The bill would also revise the requirements for entering into a domestic partnership to require each person to consent to the jurisdiction of the superior courts of this state for the purpose of a proceeding to obtain a judgment of dissolution or nullity of the domestic partnership. The bill would revise the provision described above making it a misdemeanor to violate the provision specifying the requirements for completing the form necessary to create a domestic partnership. The bill would instead specifically provide that filing an intentionally and materially false Declaration of Domestic Partnership would be punishable as a misdemeanor, thereby creating a new crime. By creating a new crime, this bill would impose a state-mandated local program.

This bill would extend the rights and duties of marriage to persons registered as domestic partners on and after January 1, 2005. The bill would provide that the superior courts shall have jurisdiction over all proceedings governing the dissolution of domestic partnerships, nullity of domestic partnerships, and legal separation of partners in domestic partnerships. These proceedings would follow the same procedures as the equivalent proceedings with respect to marriage. The bill would provide that a legal union validly formed in another jurisdiction that is substantially equivalent to a domestic partnership would be recognized as a valid domestic partnership in this state. The bill would require the Secretary of State to send a letter on 3 separate, specified occasions to the mailing address of registered domestic partners informing them of these changes, as specified. The bill would also require the Director of General Services, through the forms management center, to provide notice to state agencies, among others, that in reviewing and revising all public-use forms that refer to or use the terms spouse, husband, wife, father, mother, marriage, or marital status, that appropriate references to domestic partner, parent, or domestic partnership be included. The bill would also make related and conforming changes. The bill would further make specified provisions operative on January 1, 2005. The bill would impose a state-mandated local program by adding to the duties of county clerks.

The California Constitution requires the state to reimburse local agencies and school districts for certain costs mandated by the state. Statutory provisions establish procedures for making that reimbursement, including the creation of a State Mandates Claims Fund to pay the costs of mandates that do not exceed $1,000,000 statewide and other procedures for claims whose statewide costs exceed $1,000,000. This bill would provide that with regard to certain mandates no reimbursement is required by this act for a specified reason. With regard to any other mandates, this bill would provide that, if the Commission on State Mandates determines that the bill contains costs so mandated by the state, reimbursement for those costs shall be made pursuant to the statutory provisions noted above.

The people of the State of California do enact as follows:

SECTION 1. (a) This act is intended to help California move closer to fulfilling the promises of inalienable rights, liberty, and equality contained in Sections 1 and 7 of Article 1 of the California Constitution by providing all caring and committed couples, regardless of their gender or sexual orientation, the opportunity to obtain essential rights, protections, and benefits and to assume corresponding responsibilities, obligations, and duties and to further the state's interests in promoting table and lasting family relationships, and protecting Californians from the economic and social consequences of abandonment, separation, the death of loved ones, and other life crises.

(b) The Legislature hereby finds and declares that despite longstanding social and economic discrimination, many lesbian, gay, and bisexual Californians have formed lasting, committed, and caring relationships with persons of the same sex. These couples share lives together, participate in their communities together, and many raise children and care for other dependent family members together. Many of these couples have sought to protect each other and their family members by registering as domestic partners with the State of California and, as a result, have received certain basic legal rights. Expanding the rights and creating responsibilities of registered domestic partners would further California's interests in promoting family relationships and protecting family members during life crises, and would reduce discrimination on the bases of sex and sexual orientation in a manner consistent with the requirements of the California Constitution.

(c) This act is not intended to repeal or adversely affect any other ways in which relationships between adults may be recognized or given effect in California, or the legal consequences of those relationships, including, among other things, civil marriage, enforcement of palimony agreements, enforcement of powers of attorney, appointment of conservators or guardians, and petitions for second parent or limited consent adoption.

SEC. 2. This act shall be known and may be cited as "The California Domestic Partner Rights and Responsibilities Act of 2003."

SEC. 3. Section 297 of the Family Code is amended to read:
297. (a) Domestic partners are two adults who have chosen to share one another's lives in an intimate and committed relationship of mutual caring.
(b) A domestic partnership shall be established in California when both persons file a Declaration of Domestic Partnership with the Secretary of State pursuant to this division, and, at the time of filing, all of the following requirements are met:
(1) Both persons have a common residence.
(2) Neither person is married to someone else or is a member of another domestic partnership with someone else that has not been terminated, dissolved, or adjudged a nullity.
(3) The two persons are not related by blood in a way that would prevent them from being married to each other in this state.
(4) Both persons are at least 18 years of age.
(5) Either of the following:
(A) Both persons are members of the same sex.
(B) One or both of the persons meet the eligibility criteria under Title II of the Social Security Act as defined in 42 U.S.C. Section 402(a) for old-age insurance benefits or Title XVI of the Social Security Act as defined in 42 U.S.C. Section 1381 for aged individuals. Notwithstanding any other provision of this section, persons of opposite sexes may not constitute a domestic partnership unless one or both of the persons are over the age of 62.
(6) Both persons are capable of consenting to the domestic partnership.
(c) "Have a common residence" means that both domestic partners share the same residence. It is not necessary that the legal right to possess the common residence be in both of their names. Two people have a common residence even if one or both have additional residences. Domestic partners do not cease to have a common residence if one leaves the common residence but intends to return.

SEC. 4. Section 297.5 is added to the Family Code, to read:
297.5. (a) Registered domestic partners shall have the same rights,

protections, and benefits, and shall be subject to the same responsibilities, obligations, and duties under law, whether they derive from statutes, administrative regulations, court rules, government policies, common law, or any other provisions or sources of law, as are granted to and imposed upon spouses.

(b) Former registered domestic partners shall have the same rights, protections, and benefits, and shall be subject to the same responsibilities, obligations, and duties under law, whether they derive from statutes, administrative regulations, court rules, government policies, common law, or any other provisions or sources of law, as are granted to and imposed upon former spouses.

(c) A surviving registered domestic partner, following the death of the other partner, shall have the same rights, protections, and benefits, and shall be subject to the same responsibilities, obligations, and duties under law, whether they derive from statutes, administrative regulations, court rules, government policies, common law, or any other provisions or sources of law, as are granted to and imposed upon a widow or a widower.

(d) The rights and obligations of registered domestic partners with respect to a child of either of them shall be the same as those of spouses. The rights and obligations of former or surviving registered domestic partners with respect to a child of either of them shall be the same as those of former or surviving spouses.

(e) To the extent that provisions of California law adopt, refer to, or rely upon, provisions of federal law in a way that otherwise would cause registered domestic partners to be treated differently than spouses, registered domestic partners shall be treated by California law as if federal law recognized a domestic partnership in the same manner as California law.

(f) Registered domestic partners shall have the same rights regarding nondiscrimination as those provided to spouses.

(g) Notwithstanding this section, in filing their state income tax returns, domestic partners shall use the same filing status as is used on their federal income tax returns, or that would have been used had they filed federal income tax returns. Earned income may not be treated as community property for state income tax purposes.

(h) No public agency in this state may discriminate against any person or couple on the ground that the person is a registered domestic partner rather than a spouse or that the couple are registered domestic partners rather than spouses, except that nothing in this section applies to modify eligibility for long-term care plans pursuant to Chapter 15 (commencing with Section 21660) of Part 3 of Division 5 of Title 2 of the Government Code.

(i) This act does not preclude any state or local agency from exercising its regulatory authority to implement statutes providing rights to, or imposing responsibilities upon, domestic partners.

(j) This section does not amend or modify any provision of the California Constitution or any provision of any statute that was adopted by initiative.

(k) This section does not amend or modify federal laws or the benefits, protections, and responsibilities provided by those laws.

(l) Where necessary to implement the rights of domestic partners under this act, gender-specific terms referring to spouses shall be construed to include domestic partners.

SEC. 5. Section 298 of the Family Code is amended to read:

298. (a) The Secretary of State shall prepare forms entitled "Declaration of Domestic Partnership" and "Notice of Termination of Domestic Partnership" to meet the requirements of this division. These forms shall require the signature and seal of an acknowledgment by a notary public to be binding and valid.

(b) (1) The Secretary of State shall distribute these forms to each county clerk. These forms shall be available to the public at the office of the Secretary of State and each county clerk.

(2) The Secretary of State shall, by regulation, establish fees for the actual costs of processing each of these forms, and the cost for preparing and sending the mailings and notices required pursuant to Section 299.3, and shall charge these fees to persons filing the forms.

(c) The Declaration of Domestic Partnership shall require each person who wants to become a domestic partner to (1) state that he or she meets the requirements of Section 297 at the time the form is signed, (2) provide a mailing address, (3) state that he or she consents to the jurisdiction of the Superior Courts of California for the purpose of a proceeding to obtain a judgment of dissolution or nullity of the domestic partnership or for legal separation of partners in the domestic partnership, or for any other proceeding related to the partners' rights and obligations, even if one or both partners ceases to be a resident of, or to maintain a domicile in, this state, (4) sign the form with a declaration that representations made therein are true, correct, and contain no material omissions of fact to the best knowledge and belief of the applicant, and (5) have a notary public acknowledge his or her signature. Both partners' signatures shall be affixed to one Declaration of Domestic Partnership form, which form shall then be transmitted to the Secretary of State according to the instructions provided on the form. Filing an intentionally and materially false Declaration of Domestic Partnership shall be punishable as a misdemeanor.

SEC. 6. Section 298.5 of the Family Code is amended to read:
298.5. (a) Two persons desiring to become domestic partners may complete and file a Declaration of Domestic Partnership with the Secretary of State.
(b) The Secretary of State shall register the Declaration of Domestic Partnership in a registry for those partnerships, and shall return a copy of the registered form and a Certificate of Registered Domestic Partnership to the domestic partners at the mailing address provided by the domestic partners.
(c) No person who has filed a Declaration of Domestic Partnership may file a new Declaration of Domestic Partnership or enter a civil marriage with someone other than their registered domestic partner unless the most recent domestic partnership has been terminated or a final judgment of dissolution or nullity of the most recent domestic partnership has been entered. This prohibition does not apply if the previous domestic partnership ended because one of the partners died.

SEC. 7. Section 299 of the Family Code is repealed.

SEC. 8. Section 299 is added to the Family Code, to read:
299. (a) A domestic partnership may be terminated without filing a proceeding for dissolution of domestic partnership by the filing of a Notice of Termination of Domestic Partnership with the Secretary of State pursuant to this section, provided that all of the following conditions exist at the time of the filing:
(1) The Notice of Termination of Domestic Partnership is signed by both domestic partners.
(2) There are no children of the relationship of the parties born before or after registration of the domestic partnership or adopted by the parties after registration of the domestic partnership, and neither of the domestic partners, to their knowledge, is pregnant.
(3) The domestic partnership is not more than five years in duration.
(4) Neither party has any interest in real property wherever situated, with the exception of the lease of a residence occupied by either party which

satisfies the following requirements:
(A) The lease does not include an option to purchase.
(B) The lease terminates within one year from the date of filing of the Notice of Termination of Domestic Partnership.
(5) There are no unpaid obligations in excess of the amount described in paragraph (6) of subdivision (a) of Section 2400, as adjusted by subdivision (b) of Section 2400, incurred by either or both of the parties after registration of the domestic partnership, excluding the amount of any unpaid obligation with respect to an automobile.
(6) The total fair market value of community property assets, excluding all encumbrances and automobiles, including any deferred compensation or retirement plan, is less than the amount described in paragraph (7) of subdivision (a) of Section 2400, as adjusted by subdivision (b) of Section 2400, and neither party has separate property assets, excluding all encumbrances and automobiles, in excess of that amount.
(7) The parties have executed an agreement setting forth the division of assets and the assumption of liabilities of the community property, and have executed any documents, title certificates, bills of sale, or other evidence of transfer necessary to effectuate the agreement.
(8) The parties waive any rights to support by the other domestic partner.
(9) The parties have read and understand a brochure prepared by the Secretary of State describing the requirements, nature, and effect of terminating a domestic partnership.
(10) Both parties desire that the domestic partnership be terminated.
(b) The domestic partnership shall be terminated effective six months after the date of filing of the Notice of Termination of Domestic Partnership with the Secretary of State pursuant to this section, provided that neither party has, before that date, filed with the Secretary of State a notice of revocation of the termination of domestic partnership, in the form and content as shall be prescribed by the Secretary of State, and sent to the other party a copy of the notice of revocation by first-class mail, postage prepaid, at the other party's last known address. The effect of termination of a domestic partnership pursuant to this section shall be the same as, and shall be treated for all purposes as, the entry of a judgment of dissolution of a domestic partnership.
(c) The termination of a domestic partnership pursuant to subdivision (b) does not prejudice nor bar the rights of either of the parties to institute an action in the superior court to set aside the termination for fraud, duress, mistake, or any other ground recognized at law or in equity. A court may set aside the termination of domestic partnership and declare the

termination of the domestic partnership null and void upon proof that the parties did not meet the requirements of subdivision (a) at the time of the filing of the Notice of Termination of Domestic Partnership with the Secretary of State.
(d) The superior courts shall have jurisdiction over all proceedings relating to the dissolution of domestic partnerships, nullity of domestic partnerships, and legal separation of partners in a domestic partnership. The dissolution of a domestic partnership, nullity of a domestic partnership, and legal separation of partners in a domestic partnership shall follow the same procedures, and the partners shall possess the same rights, protections, and benefits, and be subject to the same responsibilities, obligations, and duties, as apply to the dissolution of marriage, nullity of marriage, and legal separation of spouses in a marriage, respectively, except as provided in subdivision (a), and except that, in accordance with the consent acknowledged by domestic partners in the Declaration of Domestic Partnership form, proceedings for dissolution, nullity, or legal separation of a domestic partnership registered in this state may be filed in the superior courts of this state even if neither domestic partner is a resident of, or maintains a domicile in, the state at the time the proceedings are filed.

SEC. 9. Section 299.2 is added to the Family Code, to read:
299.2. A legal union of two persons of the same sex, other than a marriage, that was validly formed in another jurisdiction, and that is substantially equivalent to a domestic partnership as defined in this part, shall be recognized as a valid domestic partnership in this state regardless of whether it bears the name domestic partnership.

SEC. 10. Section 299.3 is added to the Family Code, to read:
299.3. (a) On or before June 30, 2004, and again on or before December 1, 2004, and again on or before January 31, 2005, the Secretary of State shall send the following letter to the mailing address on file of each registered domestic partner who registered more than one month prior to each of those dates:

"Dear Registered Domestic Partner:

This letter is being sent to all persons who have registered with the

Secretary of State as a domestic partner. Effective January 1, 2005, California's law related to the rights and responsibilities of registered domestic partners will change (or, if you are receiving this letter after that date, the law has changed, as of January 1, 2005). With this new legislation, for purposes of California law, domestic partners will have a great many new rights and responsibilities, including laws governing community property, those governing property transfer, those regarding duties of mutual financial support and mutual responsibilities for certain debts to third parties, and many others. The way domestic partnerships are terminated is also changing. After January 1, 2005, under certain circumstances, it will be necessary to participate in a dissolution proceeding in court to end a domestic partnership.

Domestic partners who do not wish to be subject to these new rights and responsibilities MUST terminate their domestic partnership before January 1, 2005. Under the law in effect until January 1, 2005, your domestic partnership is automatically terminated if you or your partner marry or die while you are registered as domestic partners. It is also terminated if you send to your partner or your partner sends to you, by certified mail, a notice terminating the domestic partnership, or if you and your partner no longer share a common residence. In all cases, you are required to file a Notice of Termination of Domestic Partnership. If you do not terminate your domestic partnership before January 1, 2005, as provided above, you will be subject to these new rights and responsibilities and, under certain circumstances, you will only be able to terminate your domestic partnership, other than as a result of domestic partner's death, by the filing of a court action.

If you have any questions about any of these changes, please consult an attorney. If you cannot find an attorney in your locale, please contact your county bar association for a referral.

Sincerely,
The Secretary of State"

(b) From January 1, 2004, to December 31, 2004, inclusive, the Secretary of State shall provide the following notice with all requests for the Declaration of Domestic Partnership form. The Secretary of State also shall attach the Notice to the Declaration of Domestic Partnership form that is provided to the general public on the Secretary of State's

Web site:

"NOTICE TO POTENTIAL DOMESTIC PARTNER REGISTRANTS
As of January 1, 2005, California's law of domestic partnership will change. Beginning at that time, for purposes of California law, domestic partners will have a great many new rights and responsibilities, including laws governing community property, those governing property transfer, those regarding duties of mutual financial support and mutual responsibilities for certain debts to third parties, and many others. The way domestic partnerships are terminated will also change. Unlike current law, which allows partners to end their partnership simply by filing a "Termination of Domestic Partnership" form with the Secretary of State, after January 1, 2005, it will be necessary under certain circumstances to participate in a dissolution proceeding in court to end a domestic partnership. If you have questions about these changes, please consult an attorney. If you cannot find an attorney in your area, please contact your county bar association for a referral."

SEC. 11. Section 299.5 of the Family Code is repealed.

SEC. 12. Section 14771 of the Government Code is amended to read:
14771. (a) The director, through the forms management center, shall do all of the following:
(1) Establish a State Forms Management Program for all state agencies, and provide assistance in establishing internal forms management capabilities.
(2) Study, develop, coordinate and initiate forms of interagency and common administrative usage, and establish basic state design and specification criteria to effect the standardization of public-use forms.
(3) Provide assistance to state agencies for economical forms design and forms art work composition and establish and supervise control procedures to prevent the undue creation and reproduction of public-use forms.
(4) Provide assistance, training, and instruction in forms management techniques to state agencies, forms management representatives, and departmental forms coordinators, and provide direct administrative and forms management assistance to new state organizations as they are created.
(5) Maintain a central cross index of public-use forms to facilitate the standardization of these forms, to eliminate redundant forms, and to

provide a central source of information on the usage and availability of forms.

(6) Utilize appropriate procurement techniques to take advantage of competitive bidding, consolidated orders, and contract procurement of forms, and work directly with the Office of State Publishing toward more efficient, economical and timely procurement, receipt, storage, and distribution of state forms.

(7) Coordinate the forms management program with the existing state archives and records management program to ensure timely disposition of outdated forms and related records.

(8) Conduct periodic evaluations of the effectiveness of the overall forms management program and the forms management practices of the individual state agencies, and maintain records which indicate net dollar savings which have been realized through centralized forms management.

(9) Develop and promulgate rules and standards to implement the overall purposes of this section.

(10) Create and maintain by July 1, 1986, a complete and comprehensive inventory of public-use forms in current use by the state.

(11) Establish and maintain, by July 1, 1986, an index of all public-use forms in current use by the state.

(12) Assign, by January 1, 1987, a control number to all public-use forms in current use by the state.

(13) Establish a goal to reduce the existing burden of state collections of public information by 30 percent by July 1, 1987, and to reduce that burden by an additional 15 percent by July 1, 1988.

(14) Provide notice to state agencies, forms management representatives, and departmental forms coordinators, that in the usual course of reviewing and revising all public-use forms that refer to or use the terms spouse, husband, wife, father, mother, marriage, or marital status, that appropriate references to domestic partner, parent, or domestic partnership are to be included.

(15) Delegate implementing authority to state agencies where the delegation will result in the most timely and economical method of accomplishing the responsibilities set forth in this section. The director, through the forms management center, may require any agency to revise any public-use form which the director determines is inefficient.

(b) Due to the need for tax forms to be available to the public on a timely basis, all tax forms, including returns, schedules, notices, and instructions prepared by the Franchise Tax Board for public use in connection with its

administration of the Personal Income Tax Law, Senior Citizens Property Tax Assistance and Postponement Law, Bank and Corporation Tax Law, and the Political Reform Act of 1974 and the State Board of Equalization's administration of county assessment standards, state-assessed property, timber tax, sales and use tax, hazardous substances tax, alcoholic beverage tax, cigarette tax, motor vehicle fuel license tax, use fuel tax, energy resources surcharge, emergency telephone users surcharge, insurance tax, and universal telephone service tax shall be exempt from subdivision (a), and, instead, each board shall do all of the following:
(1) Establish a goal to standardize, consolidate, simplify, efficiently manage, and, where possible, reduce the number of tax forms.
(2) Create and maintain, by July 1, 1986, a complete and comprehensive inventory of tax forms in current use by the board.
(3) Establish and maintain, by July 1, 1986, an index of all tax forms in current use by the board.
(4) Report to the Legislature, by January 1, 1987, on its progress to improve the effectiveness and efficiency of all tax forms.
(c) The director, through the forms management center, shall develop and maintain, by December 31, 1995, an ongoing master inventory of all nontax reporting forms required of businesses by state agencies, including a schedule for notifying each state agency of the impending expiration of certain report review requirements pursuant to subdivision (b) of Section 14775.

SEC. 13. Section 3 of Chapter 447 of the Statutes of 2002 is amended to read:
Sec. 3. On or before March 1, 2003, the Secretary of State shall send the following letter to the mailing address on file of each registered domestic partner who registered prior to January 1, 2003:

"Dear Registered Domestic Partner:
This letter is being sent to all persons who have registered with the Secretary of State as a domestic partner. As of July 1, 2003, California's law of intestate succession will change. The intestate succession law specifies what happens to a person's property when that person dies without a will, trust, or other estate plan.

Under existing law, if a domestic partner dies without a will, trust, or other estate plan, a surviving domestic partner cannot inherit any of the deceased partner's separate property. Instead, surviving relatives, including, for example, children, brothers, sisters, nieces, nephews, or parents may inherit the deceased partner's separate property.

Under the law to take effect July 1, 2003, if a domestic partner dies without a will, trust, or other estate plan, the surviving domestic partner will inherit the deceased partner's separate property in the same manner as a surviving spouse. This change will mean that the surviving domestic partner would inherit a third, a half, or all of the deceased partner's separate property, depending on whether the deceased domestic partner has surviving children or other relatives. This change does not affect any community or quasi-community property that the deceased partner may have had. This change in the intestate succession law will not affect you if you have a will, trust, or other estate plan. If you do not have a will, trust, or other estate plan and you do not wish to have your domestic partner inherit your separate property in the manner provided by the revised law, you may prepare a will, trust, or other estate plan, or terminate your domestic partnership.

Under existing law, your domestic partnership is automatically terminated if you or your partner married or died while you were registered as domestic partners. It is also terminated by you sending your partner or your partner sending to you by certified mail a notice terminating the domestic partnership, or by you and your partner no longer sharing a common residence. In all cases, you are required to file a Notice of Termination of Domestic Partnership with the Secretary of State in order to establish the actual date of termination of the domestic partnership. You can obtain a Notice of Termination of Domestic Partnership from the Secretary of State's office. If your domestic partnership has terminated because you sent your partner or your partner sent to you a notice of termination of your domestic partnership, you must immediately file a Notice of Termination of Domestic Partnership. If you do not file that notice, your former domestic partner may inherit under the new law. However, if your domestic partnership has terminated because you or your partner married or you and your partner no longer share a common residence, neither you nor your former partner may inherit from the other under this new law.

If you have any questions about this change, please consult an estate planning attorney. If you cannot find an estate planning attorney in your locale, please contact your county bar association for a referral.

Sincerely,
The Secretary of State"

SEC. 14. The provisions of Sections 3, 4, 5, 6, 7, 8, 9, and 11 of this act shall become operative on January 1, 2005.

SEC. 15. This act shall be construed liberally in order to secure to eligible couples who register as domestic partners the full range of legal rights, protections and benefits, as well as all of the responsibilities, obligations, and duties to each other, to their children, to third parties and to the state, as the laws of California extend to and impose upon spouses.

SEC. 16. The provisions of this act are severable. If any provision of this act is held to be invalid, or if any application thereof to any person or circumstance is held to be invalid, the invalidity shall not affect other provisions or applications that may be given effect without the invalid provision or application.

SEC. 17. No reimbursement is required by this act pursuant to Section 6 of Article XIII B of the California Constitution for certain costs that may be incurred by a local agency or school district because in that regard this act creates a new crime or infraction, eliminates a crime or infraction, or changes the penalty for a crime or infraction, within the meaning of Section 17556 of the Government Code, or changes the definition of a crime within the meaning of Section 6 of Article XIII B of the California Constitution. However, notwithstanding Section 17610 of the Government Code, if the Commission on State Mandates determines that this act contains other costs mandated by the state, reimbursement to local agencies and school districts for those costs shall be made pursuant to Part 7 (commencing with Section 17500) of Division 4 of Title 2 of the Government Code. If the statewide cost of the claim for reimbursement does not exceed one million dollars ($1,000,000), reimbursement shall be made from the State Mandates Claims Fund.

APPENDIX B

THE CALIFORNIA CODES

Business & Professions Code
Civil Code
Code of Civil Procedure
Corporations Code
Education Code
Elections Code
Evidence Code
Family Code
Financial Code
Fish and Game Code
Food and Agricultural Code
Government Code
Harbors and Navigation Code
Health and Safety Code
Insurance Code
Labor Code
Military and Veterans Code
Penal Code
Probate Code
Public Contract Code
Public Resources Code
Public Utilities Code
Revenue and Taxation Code
Streets and Highways Code
Unemployment Insurance Code
Uniform Commercial Code
Vehicle Code
Water Code
Welfare and Institutions Code

APPENDIX C

AMERICAN PSYCHOLOGICAL ASSOCIATION
Resolution on Sexual Orientation and Marriage
(July 28, 2004)

Research Summary

Minority Stress in Lesbian, Gay, and Bisexual Individuals

Psychological and psychiatric experts have agreed since 1975 that homosexuality is neither a form of mental illness nor a symptom of mental illness (Conger, 1975). Nonetheless, there is growing recognition that social prejudice, discrimination, and violence against lesbians, gay men, and bisexuals take a cumulative toll on the well-being of these individuals. Researchers (e.g., DiPlacido, 1998; Meyer, 2003) use the term "minority stress" to refer to the negative effects associated with the adverse social conditions experienced by individuals who belong to a stigmatized social group (e.g., the elderly, members of racial and ethnic minority groups, the physically disabled, women, the poor or those on welfare, or individuals who are gay, lesbian, or bisexual).

A recent meta-analysis of population-based epidemiological studies showed that lesbian, gay, and bisexual populations have higher rates of stress-related psychiatric disorders (such as those related to anxiety, mood, and substance use) than do heterosexual populations (Meyer, 2003). These differences are not large but are relatively consistent across studies (e.g., Cochran & Mays, 2000; Cochran, Sullivan, & Mays, 2003; Gilman et al., 2001; Mays & Cochran, 2001). Meyer also provided evidence that within lesbian, gay, and bisexual populations, those who more frequently felt stigmatized or discriminated against because of their sexual orientation, who had to conceal their homosexuality, or who were prevented from affiliating with other lesbian, gay, or bisexual individuals tended to report more frequent mental health concerns. Research also shows that compared to heterosexual individuals and couples, gay and lesbian individuals and couples experience economic disadvantages (e.g., Badgett, 2001). Finally, the violence associated with hate crimes puts lesbians, gay men and bisexual individuals at risk for physical harm to themselves, their families, and their property (D'Augelli, 1998; Herek, Gillis, & Cogan, 1999). Taken together, the evidence clearly supports the position that the social stigma, prejudice, discrimination, and violence associated with not having a heterosexual sexual orientation and the hostile and stressful social environments created thereby adversely affect the psychological, physical, social, and economic well-being of lesbian, gay, and bisexual individuals.

Same-Sex Couples

Research indicates that many gay men and lesbians want and have committed relationships. For example, survey data indicate that between 40% and 60% of gay men and between 45% and 80% of lesbians are currently involved in a romantic relationship (e.g., Bradford, Ryan, & Rothblum, 1994; Falkner & Garber, 2002; Morris, Balsam, & Rothblum, 2002). Further, data from the 2000 United States Census (United States Census Bureau, 2000) indicate that of the 5.5 million couples who were living together but not married, about 1 in 9 (594,391) had partners of the same sex. Although the Census data are almost certainly an underestimate of the actual number of cohabiting same-sex couples, they indicated that a male householder and a male partner headed 301,026 households and that a female householder and a female partner headed 293,365 households.[3] Despite persuasive evidence that gay men and lesbians have committed relationships, three concerns about same-sex couples are often raised. A first concern is that the contrary, relationships of gay men and lesbians are dysfunctional and unhappy. To the studies that have compared partners from same-sex couples to partners from heterosexual couples on standardized measures of relationship quality (such as satisfaction and commitment) have found partners from same-sex and heterosexual couples to be equivalent to each other (see reviews by Peplau & Beals, 2004; Peplau & Spalding, 2000).

A second concern is that the relationships of gay men and lesbians are

---

[3] The same-sex couples identified in the U.S. Census may include couples in which one or both partners are bisexually identified, rather than gay or lesbian identified.

unstable. However, research indicates that, despite the somewhat hostile social climate within which same-sex relationships develop, many lesbians and gay men have formed durable relationships. For example, survey data indicate that between 18% and 28% of gay couples and between 8% and 21 % of lesbian couples have lived together 10 or more years (e.g., Blumstein & Schwartz, 1983; Bryant & Demian, 1994; Falkner & Garber, 2002; Kurdek, 2003). Researchers (e.g., Kurdek, in press) have also speculated that the stability of same-sex couples would be enhanced if partners from same-sex couples enjoyed the same levels of social support and public recognition of their relationships as partners from heterosexual couples do.

A third concern is that the processes that affect the well-being and permanence of the relationships of lesbian and gay persons are different from those that affect the relationships of heterosexual persons. In fact, research has found that the factors that predict relationship satisfaction, relationship commitment, and relationship stability are remarkably similar for both same-sex cohabiting couples and heterosexual married couples (Kurdek, 2001, in press).

Resolution

WHEREAS APA has a long-established policy to deplore "all public and private discrimination against gay men and lesbians" and urges "the repeal of all discriminatory legislation against lesbians and gay men" (Conger, 1975, p. 633);

WHEREAS the APA adopted the Resolution on Legal Benefits for Same-Sex Couples in 1998 (Levant, 1998, pp. 665-666);

WHEREAS Discrimination and prejudice based on sexual orientation detrimentally affects psychological, physical, social, and economic well-being (Badgett, 2001; Cochran, Sullivan, & Mays, 2003; Herek, Gillis, & Cogan, 1999; Meyer; 2003);

WHEREAS "Anthropological research on households, kinship relationships, and families, across cultures and through time, provides no support whatsoever for the view that either civilization or viable social orders depend upon marriage as an exclusively heterosexual institution" (American Anthropological Association, 2004);

WHEREAS Psychological research on relationships and couples provides no evidence to justify discrimination against same-sex couples (Kurdek, 2001, in press; Peplau & Beals, 2004; Peplau & Spalding, 2000);

WHEREAS The institution of civil marriage confers a social status[4] and important legal benefits, rights, and privileges;[5]

WHEREAS The United States General Accounting Office (2004) has identified over 1,000 federal statutory provisions in which marital

---

[4] Turner v. Safley, 482 U.S. 78, 95-96 (1987) (summarizing intangible social benefits of marriage in the course of striking down state restrictions on prisoner marriage, "[m]arriages . . . are expressions of emotional support and public commitment. These elements are an important and significant aspect of the marital relationship."); Maynard v. Hill, 125 U.S. 190, 211 (1888) (marriage is more than a mere contract, it is "the foundation of the family and of society"); Goodridge v. Dep't of Public Health, 798 N.E.2d 941 (Mass. 2003) ("[m]arriage also bestows enormous private and social advantages on those who choose to marry. Civil marriage is at once a deeply personal commitment to another human being and a highly public celebration of the ideals of mutuality, companionship, intimacy, fidelity, and family"); James M. Donovan, Same-Sex Union Announcements: Whether Newspapers Must Publish Them, and Why Should we Care, 68 BROOK. L. REV. 721, 746 (2003) ("the intangible benefit of public recognition is arguably the most important benefit of marriage to the couple as a unit"); Gil Kujovich, An Essay on the Passive Virtue of Baker v. State, 25 VT. L. REV. 93, 96 (2000) ("historically, marriage has been the only state-sanctioned and socially approved means by which two people commit themselves to each other. It has been the most favored context for forming a family and raising children. From this perspective, creation of a same-sex alternative to marriage amounts to an exclusion from the preferred and accepted status---an exclusion that could imply the inferiority or unworthiness of the couples who are excluded, even if the alternative confers precisely the same tangible benefits and protections as marriage."); Greg Johnson, Vermont Civil Unions: The New Language of Marriage, 25 Vt. L. Rev. 15, 17 (2000) (reflecting on the inferior status of civil unions as compared to marriage).

[5] See e.g., Goodridge v. Dep't of Public Health, 798 N.E.2d 941, 955-958 (Mass. 2003) (outlining Massachusetts statutory benefits and rights previously available only to married persons); Baker v. State, 744 A.2d 864, 883-84 (Vt. 1999) (outlining Vermont statutory benefits and rights previously available only to married persons); Baehr v. Lewin, 852 P.2d 44, 59 (Haw. 1993) (summarizing some of the state law benefits available only to married persons in Hawaii).

status is a factor in determining or receiving benefits, rights, and privileges, for example, those concerning taxation, federal loans, and dependent and survivor benefits (e.g., Social Security, military, and veterans);

WHEREAS There are numerous state, local, and private sector laws and other provisions in which marital status is a factor in determining or receiving benefits, rights, and privileges, for example, those concerning taxation, health insurance, health care decision-making, property rights, pension and retirement benefits, and inheritance;[6]

WHEREAS Same-sex couples are denied equal access to civil marriage;[7]

WHEREAS Same-sex couples who enter into a civil union are denied equal access to all the benefits, rights, and privileges provided by federal law to married couples (United States General Accounting Office, 2004);[8]

WHEREAS The benefits, rights, and privileges associated with domestic partnerships are not universally available,[9] are not equal to those

---

[6] See Note 3.

[7] William N. Eskridge, Jr., Gaylaw: Challenging the apartheid of the closet 134-35 (1999) (describing the continuing exclusion of gays and lesbians from civil marriage).

[8] William N. Eskridge, Jr., Equality Practice: Liberal Reflections on the Jurisprudence of Civil Unions, 64 ALB. L. REV. 853, 861-62 (2001) (describing the "unequal benefits and obligations" of civil unions under federal law) ; Mark Strasser, Mission Impossible: On Baker, Equal Benefits, and the Imposition of Stigma, 9 WM. & MARY BILL RTS. J. 1, 22 (2000) ("[S]ame-sex civil union partners still would not be entitled to federal marital benefits . . . ."); Recent Legislation, Act Relating to Civil Unions, 114 HARV. L. REV. 1421, 1423 (2001) ("Furthermore, the parallel between civil unions and marriage extends only to those aspects of each that do not implicate federal law. As the 'Construction' section of ARCU [the Act Relating to Civil Union] acknowledges, '[m]any of the laws of [Vermont] are intertwined with federal law, and the general assembly recognizes that it does not have the jurisdiction to control federal laws or the benefits, protections and responsibilities related to them.'").

[9] Gary D. Allison, Sanctioning Sodomy: The Supreme Court Liberates Gay Sex and Limits State Power To Vindicate the Moral Sentiments of the People, 39 TULSA L. REV. 95, 137 (2003) ("Currently, eight states have

associated with marriage[10] and are rarely portable;[11]

WHEREAS people who also experience discrimination based on age, race, ethnicity, disability, gender and gender identity, religion, and socioeconomic status may especially benefit from access to marriage for same-sex couples (Division 44/Committee on Lesbian, Gay, and Bisexual Concerns Joint Task Force on Guidelines for Psychotherapy with Lesbian, Gay, and Bisexual Clients, 2000);

THEREFORE BE IT RESOLVED That the APA believes that it is unfair and discriminatory to deny same-sex couples legal access to civil marriage and to all its attendant benefits, rights, and privileges;

THEREFORE BE IT FURTHER RESOLVED That APA shall take a leadership role in opposing all discrimination in legal benefits, rights, and privileges against same-sex couples;

THEREFORE BE IT FURTHER RESOLVED That APA encourages psychologists to act to eliminate all discrimination against same-sex couples in their practice, research, education and training ("Ethical Principles," 2002, p. 1063);

THEREFORE BE IT FURTHER RESOLVED That the APA shall provide scientific and educational resources that inform public discussion and

---

domestic partnership laws in place. By the late 1990s, 421 cities and states, and over 3,500 businesses or institutions of higher education offered some form of domestic partner benefit.") (citations and internal quotations omitted).

[10] Eileen Shin, Same-Sex Unions and Domestic Partnership, 4 GEO. J. GENDER & L. 261, 272-78 (2002) (describing the limited reach of various domestic partnership laws); Mark Strasser, Some Observations about DOMA, Marriages, Civil Unions, and Domestic Partnerships , 30 CAP. U. L. REV. 363, 381 (2002) (noting that while domestic partnerships "provide particular financial benefits" and offer "a vehicle whereby individuals can express that they have a particular kind of relationship with someone else," they "are neither the equivalent of civil unions nor the equivalent of marriage").

[11] Nancy J. Knauer, The September 11 Attacks and Surviving Same-Sex Partners: Defining Family Through Tragedy, 75 TEMP. L. REV. 31, 93 (2002) ("The two major drawbacks of domestic partnership are that it tends to grant relatively few rights and it is almost never portable.").

public policy development regarding sexual orientation and marriage and that assist its members, divisions, and affiliated state, provincial, and territorial psychological associations.

References

American Anthropological Association. (2004). Statement on marriage and family from the American Anthropological Association. Retrieved May 11, 2004, from http://www.aaanet.org/press/ma stmt marriage.htm.

Badgett, M. V. L. (2001). Money, myths, and change: The economic lives of lesbians and gay men. Chicago: University of Chicago Press.

Blumstein, P., & Schwartz, P. (1983). American couples: Money, work, sex. New York: William Morrow and Company, Inc.

Bradford, J., Ryan, C., & Rothblum, E. D. (1994). National lesbian health care survey: Implications for mental health care. Journal of Consulting and Clinical Psychology, 62, 228-242.

Bryant, A. S., & Demian. (1994). Relationship characteristics of gay and lesbian couples: Findings from a national survey. Journal of Gay and Lesbian Social Services, 1, 101-117.

Cochran, S. D., & Mays, V. M. (2000). Relation between psychiatric syndromes and behaviorally defined sexual orientation in a sample of the US population. Journal of Epidemiology, 151, 516-523.

Cochran, S. D., Sullivan, J. G., & Mays, V. M. (2003). Prevalence of mental disorders, psychological distress, and mental health service use among lesbian, gay, and bisexual adults in the United States. Journal of Consulting and Clinical Psychology, 71, 53-61.

Conger, J. J. (1975). Proceedings of the American Psychological Association, Incorporated, for the year 1974: Minutes of the annual meeting of the Council of Representatives. American Psychologist, 30, 620-651.

D'Augelli, A. R. (1998). Developmental implications of victimization of lesbian, gay, and bisexual youths. In G.M. Herek (Ed.), Stigma and sexual orientation: Understanding prejudice against lesbians, gay men, and bisexuals (pp. 187-210). Thousand Oaks, CA: Sage.

DiPlacido, J. (1998). Minority stress among lesbians, gay men, and bisexuals: A consequence of heterosexism, homophobia, and stigmatization. In G. M. Herek (Ed.), Stigma and sexual orientation (pp. 138-159). Thousand Oaks, CA: Sage.

Division 44/Committee on Lesbian, Gay, and Bisexual Concerns Joint Task Force on Guidelines for Psychotherapy with Lesbian, Gay, and Bisexual Clients. (2000). Guidelines for Psychotherapy with Lesbian, Gay, and Bisexual Clients. American Psychologist, 55, 1440-1451.

Ethical Principles of Psychologists and Code of Conduct. (2002). American Psychologist, 57, 1060-1073.

Gilman, S. E., Cochran, S. D., Mays, V. M., Hughes, M., Ostrow, D., & Kessler, R. C. (2001). Risks of psychiatric disorders among individuals reporting same-sex sexual partners in the National Comorbidity Survey. American Journal of Public Health, 91, 933-939.

Falkner, A., & Garber, J. (2002). 2001 gay/lesbian consumer online census. Syracuse, NY: Syracuse University, OpusComm Group, and GSociety.

Herek, G. M., Gillis, J. R., & Cogan, J. C. (1999). Psychological sequelae of hate crime victimization among lesbian, gay, and bisexual adults. Journal of Consulting and Clinical Psychology, 67, 945-951.

Kurdek, L. A. (2001). Differences between heterosexual non-parent couples and gay, lesbian, and heterosexual parent couples. Journal of Family Issues, 22, 727-754.

Kurdek, L. A. (2003). Differences between gay and lesbian cohabiting couples. Journal of Social Personal Relationships, 20, 411-436.

Kurdek, L. A. (in press). Are gay and lesbian cohabiting couples really different from heterosexual married couples? Journal of Marriage and Family.

Levant, R. F. (1999). Proceedings of the American Psychological Association, Incorporated, for the legislative year 1998: Minutes of the Annual Meeting of the Council of Representatives, February 20-22, 1998, Washington, DC, and August 13 and 16, 1998, San Francisco, CA, and Minutes of the February, June, August, and December meetings of the Board of Directors. American Psychologist, 54, 605-671.

Mays, V. M., & Cochran, S. D. (2001). Mental health correlates of perceived discrimination among lesbian, gay, and bisexual adults in the United States. American Journal of Public Health, 91, 1869-1876.

Meyer, I. H. (2003). Prejudice, social stress, and mental

health in lesbian, gay, and bisexual populations: Conceptual issues and research evidence. Psychological Bulletin, 129, 674-697.

Morris, J. F., Balsam, K. F., & Rothblum, E. D. (2002). Lesbian and bisexual mothers and nonmothers: Demographics and the coming-out process. Developmental Psychology, 16, 144156.

Peplau, L. A., & Beals, K. P. (2004). The family lives of lesbians and gay men. In A. L. Vangelisti (Ed.), Handbook of family communication (pp. 233-248). Mahwah, NJ: Erlbaum.

Peplau, L. A., & Spalding, L. R. (2000). The close relationships of lesbians, gay men, and bisexuals. In C. Hendrick & S. S. Hendrick (Eds.), Close relationships: A sourcebook (pp. 111123). Thousand Oaks: Sage.

United States Census Bureau. (2000). Summary File 1: 2000 Census of Population and Housing. Washington, DC: US Census Bureau.

United States General Accounting Office. (2004, January 23). Defense of Marriage Act: Update to Prior Report [GAO-04-353R]. Retrieved May 19, 2004, from http://www.gao.gov

Resolution on Sexual Orientation, Parents, and Children

Research Summary

Lesbian and Gay Parents

Many lesbians and gay men are parents. In the 2000 U. S. Census, 33% of female same-sex couple households and 22% of male same-sex couple households reported at least one child under the age of 18 living in the home. Despite the significant presence of at least 163,879 households headed by lesbian or gay parents in U.S. society, three major concerns about lesbian and gay parents are commonly voiced (Falk, 1994; Patterson, Fulcher & Wainright, 2002). These include concerns that lesbians and gay men are mentally ill, that lesbians are less maternal than heterosexual women, and that lesbians' and gay men's relationships with their sexual partners leave little time for their relationships with their children. In general, research has failed to provide a basis for any of these concerns (Patterson, 2000, 2004a; Perrin, 2002; Tasker, 1999; Tasker & Golombok, 1997). First, homosexuality is not a psychological disorder (Conger, 1975). Although exposure to prejudice and discrimination based on sexual orientation may cause acute distress (Mays & Cochran, 2001; Meyer, 2003), there is no reliable evidence that homosexual orientation per se impairs psychological functioning. Second, beliefs that lesbian and gay adults are not fit parents have no empirical foundation (Patterson, 2000, 2004a; Perrin, 2002). Lesbian and heterosexual women have not been found to differ markedly in their approaches to child rearing (Patterson, 2000; Tasker, 1999). Members of gay and lesbian couples with children have been found to divide the work involved in childcare evenly, and to be satisfied with their relationships with their partners (Patterson, 2000, 2004a). The results of some studies suggest that lesbian mothers' and gay fathers' parenting skills may be superior to those of matched heterosexual parents. There is no scientific basis for concluding that lesbian mothers or gay fathers are unfit parents on the basis of their sexual orientation (Armesto, 2002; Patterson, 2000; Tasker & Golombok, 1997). On the contrary, results of research suggest that lesbian and gay parents are as likely as heterosexual parents to provide supportive and healthy environments for their children.

Children of Lesbian and Gay Parents

As the social visibility and legal status of lesbian and gay parents has increased, three major concerns about the influence of lesbian and gay parents on children have been often voiced](Falk, 1994; Patterson, Fulcher & Wainright, 2002). One is that the children of lesbian and gay parents will experience more difficulties in the area of sexual identity than children of heterosexual parents. For instance, one such concern is that children brought up by lesbian mothers or gay fathers will show disturbances in gender identity and/or in gender role behavior. A second category of concerns involves aspects of children's personal development other than sexual identity. For example, some observers have expressed fears that children in the custody of gay or lesbian parents would be more vulnerable to mental breakdown, would exhibit more adjustment difficulties and behavior problems, or would be less psychologically healthy than other children. A third category of concerns is that children of lesbian and gay parents will experience difficulty in social relationships. For example, some observers have expressed concern that children living with lesbian mothers or gay fathers will be stigmatized, teased, or otherwise victimized by peers. Another common fear is that children living with gay or lesbian parents will be more likely to be sexually abused by the parent or by the parent's friends or acquaintances.

Results of social science research have failed to confirm any of these concerns about children of lesbian and gay parents (Patterson, 2000, 2004a; Perrin, 2002; Tasker, 1999). Research suggests that sexual identities (including gender identity, gender-role behavior, and sexual orientation) develop in much the same ways among children of lesbian mothers as they do among children of heterosexual parents (Patterson, 2004a). Studies of other aspects of personal development (including personality, self-concept, and conduct) similarly reveal few differences between children of lesbian mothers and children of heterosexual parents (Perrin, 2002; Stacey & Biblarz, 2001; Tasker, 1999). However, few data regarding these concerns are available for children of gay fathers (Patterson, 2004b). Evidence also suggests that children of lesbian and gay parents have normal social relationships with peers and adults (Patterson, 2000, 2004a; Perrin, 2002; Stacey & Biblarz, 2001; Tasker, 1999; Tasker & Golombok, 1997). The picture that emerges from research is one of general engagement in social life with peers, parents, family members, and friends. Fears about children of lesbian or gay parents being sexually abused by adults, ostracized by peers, or isolated in single-sex lesbian or gay communities have received no scientific support. Overall, results of research suggest that the development, adjustment, and well-being of children with lesbian and gay parents do not differ markedly from that of children with heterosexual parents.

Resolution

WHEREAS APA supports policy and legislation that promote safe, secure, and nurturing environments for all children (DeLeon, 1993, 1995; Fox, 1991; Levant, 2000);

WHEREAS APA has a long-established policy to deplore "all public and private discrimination against gay men and lesbians" and urges "the repeal of all discriminatory legislation against lesbians and gay men" (Conger, 1975);

WHEREAS the APA adopted the Resolution on Child Custody and Placement in 1976 (Conger, 1977, p. 432)

WHEREAS Discrimination against lesbian and gay parents deprives their children of benefits, rights, and privileges enjoyed by children of heterosexual married couples;

WHEREAS some jurisdictions prohibit gay and lesbian individuals and same-sex couples from adopting children, notwithstanding the great need for adoptive parents (Lofton v. Secretary, 2004);

WHEREAS There is no scientific evidence that parenting effectiveness is related to parental sexual orientation: lesbian and gay parents are as likely as heterosexual parents to provide supportive and healthy environments for their children (Patterson, 2000, 2004; Perrin, 2002; Tasker, 1999);

WHEREAS Research has shown that the adjustment, development, and psychological well-being of children is unrelated to parental sexual orientation and that the children of lesbian and gay parents are as likely as those of heterosexual parents to flourish (Patterson, 2004; Perrin, 2002; Stacey & Biblarz, 2001);

THEREFORE BE IT RESOLVED That the APA opposes any discrimination based on sexual orientation in matters of adoption, child custody and visitation, foster care, and reproductive health services;

THEREFORE BE IT FURTHER RESOLVED That the APA believes that children reared by a same-sex couple benefit from legal ties to each parent;

THEREFORE BE IT FURTHER RESOLVED That the APA supports the protection of parent-child relationships through the legalization of joint adoptions and second parent adoptions of children being reared by same-sex couples;

THEREFORE BE IT FURTHER RESOLVED That APA shall take a leadership role in opposing all discrimination based on sexual orientation in matters of adoption, child custody and visitation, foster care, and reproductive health services;

THEREFORE BE IT FURTHER RESOLVED That APA encourages psychologists to act to eliminate all discrimination based on sexual orientation in matters of adoption, child custody and visitation, foster care, and reproductive health services in their practice, research, education and training ("Ethical Principles," 2002, p. 1063);

THEREFORE BE IT FURTHER RESOLVED That the APA shall provide scientific and educational resources that inform public discussion and public policy development regarding discrimination based on sexual orientation in matters of adoption, child custody and visitation, foster care, and reproductive health services and that assist its members, divisions, and affiliated state, provincial, and territorial psychological associations.

References

Armesto, J. C. (2002). Developmental and contextual factors that influence gay fathers' parental competence: A review of the literature. Psychology of Men and Masculinity, 3, 67 - 78.

Conger, J.J. (1975). Proceedings of the American Psychological Association,
Incorporated, for the year 1974: Minutes of the Annual meeting of the Council of Representatives. American Psychologist, 30, 620-651.

Conger, J. J. (1977). Proceedings of the American Psychological Association, Incorporated, for the legislative year 1976: Minutes of the Annual Meeting of the Council of Representatives. American Psychologist, 32, 408-438.

Fox, R.E. (1991). Proceedings of the American Psychological Association, Incorporated, for the year 1990: Minutes of the annual meeting of the Council of Representatives August 9 and 12, 1990, Boston, MA, and February 8-9, 1991, Washington, DC. American Psychologist, 45, 845.

DeLeon, P.H. (1993). Proceedings of the American Psychological Association, Incorporated, for the year 1992: Minutes of the annual meeting of the Council of Representatives August 13 and 16, 1992, and February 26-28, 1993, Washington, DC. American Psychologist, 48,782.

DeLeon, P.H. (1995). Proceedings of the American Psychological Association, Incorporated, for the year 1994: Minutes of the annual meeting of the Council of Representatives August 11 and 14, 1994, Los Angeles, CA, and February 17-19, 1995,

Washington, DC. American Psychologist, 49, 627-628.

Ethical Principles of Psychologists and Code of Conduct. (2002). American Psychologist, 57, 1060-1073.

Levant, R.F. (2000). Proceedings of the American Psychological Association, Incorporated, for the Legislative Year 1999: Minutes of the Annual Meeting of the Council of Representatives February 19-21, 1999, Washington, DC, and August 19 and 22, 1999, Boston, MA, and Minutes of the February, June, August, and December 1999 Meetings of the Board of Directors. American Psychologist, 55, 832-890.

Lofton v. Secretary of Department of Children & Family Services, 358 F.3d 804 (11th Cir. 2004).

Mays, V. M., & Cochran, S. D. (2001). Mental health correlates of perceived discrimination among lesbian, gay, and bisexual adults in the United States. American Journal of Public Health, 91, 1869-1876.

Meyer, I. H. (2003). Prejudice, social stress, and mental health in lesbian, gay, and bisexual populations: Conceptual issues and research evidence. Psychological Bulletin, 129, 674-697.

Patterson, C.J. (2000). Family relationships of lesbians and gay men. Journal of Marriage and Family, 62, 1052- 1069.

Patterson, C.J. (2004a). Lesbian and gay parents and their children: Summary of research findings. In Lesbian and gay parenting: A resource for psychologists. Washington, DC: American Psychological Association.

Patterson, C. J. (2004b). Gay fathers. In M. E. Lamb (Ed.), The role of the father in child development (4th Ed.). New York: John Wiley.

Patterson, C. J., Fulcher, M., & Wainright, J. (2002). Children of lesbian and gay parents: Research, law, and policy. In B. L. Bottoms, M. B. Kovera, and B. D. McAuliff (Eds.), Children, Social Science and the Law (pp, 176 - 199). New York: Cambridge University Press.

Perrin, E. C., and the Committee on Psychosocial Aspects of Child and Family Health (2002). Technical Report: Coparent or second-parent adoption by same-sex parents. Pediatrics, 109, 341 - 344.

Stacey, J. & Biblarz, T.J. (2001). (How) Does sexual orientation of parents matter? American Sociological Review, 65, 159-183.

Tasker, F. (1999). Children in lesbian-led families - A review. Clinical Child Psychology and Psychiatry, 4, 153 - 166.

Tasker, F., & Golombok, S. (1997). Growing up in a lesbian family. New York: Guilford Press.

APPENDIX D

SPOUSAL PRIVILEGE

CALIFORNIA EVIDENCE CODE
DIVISION 8. Privileges
CHAPTER 4. Particular Privileges
ARTICLE 4. Privilege Not To Testify Against Spouse

§ 970. Privilege not to testify against spouse
Except as otherwise provided by statute, a married person has a privilege not to testify against his spouse in any proceeding.

§ 971. Privilege not to be called as a witness against spouse
Except as otherwise provided by statute, a married person whose spouse is a party to a proceeding has a privilege not to be called as a witness by an adverse party to that proceeding without the prior express consent of the spouse having the privilege under this section unless the party calling the spouse does so in good faith without knowledge of the marital relationship.

§ 972. When privilege not applicable
A married person does not have a privilege under this article in:

(a) A proceeding brought by or on behalf of one spouse against the other spouse.

(b) A proceeding to commit or otherwise place his or her spouse or his or her spouse's property, or both, under the control of another because of the spouse's alleged mental or physical condition.

(c) A proceeding brought by or on behalf of a spouse to establish his or her competence.

(d) A proceeding under the Juvenile Court Law, Chapter 2 (commencing with Section 200) of Part 1 of Division 2 of the Welfare and Institutions Code.

(e) A criminal proceeding in which one spouse is charged with:

(1) A crime against the person or property of the other spouse or of a child, parent, relative, or cohabitant of either, whether committed before

or during marriage.

(2) A crime against the person or property of a third person committed in the course of committing a crime against the person or property of the other spouse, whether committed before or during marriage.

(3) Bigamy.

(4) A crime defined by Section 270 or 270a of the Penal Code.

(f) A proceeding resulting from a criminal act which occurred prior to legal marriage of the spouses to each other regarding knowledge acquired prior to that marriage if prior to the legal marriage the witness spouse was aware that his or her spouse had been arrested for or had been formally charged with the crime or crimes about which the spouse is called to testify.

(g) A proceeding brought against the spouse by a former spouse so long as the property and debts of the marriage have not been adjudicated, or in order to establish, modify, or enforce a child, family or spousal support obligation arising from the marriage to the former spouse; in a proceeding brought against a spouse by the other parent in order to establish, modify, or enforce a child support obligation for a child of a nonmarital relationship of the spouse; or in a proceeding brought against a spouse by the guardian of a child of that spouse in order to establish, modify, or enforce a child support obligation of the spouse. The married person does not have a privilege under this subdivision to refuse to provide information relating to the issues of income, expenses, assets, debts, and employment of either spouse, but may assert the privilege as otherwise provided in this article if other information is requested by the former spouse, guardian, or other parent of the child.

Any person demanding the otherwise privileged information made available by this subdivision, who also has an obligation to support the child for whom an order to establish, modify, or enforce child support is sought, waives his or her marital privilege to the same extent as the spouse as provided in this subdivision.

§ 973. Waiver of privilege

(a) Unless erroneously compelled to do so, a married person who testifies in a proceeding to which his spouse is a party, or who testifies against his spouse in any proceeding, does not have a privilege under this article in the proceeding in which such testimony is given.

(b) There is no privilege under this article in a civil proceeding brought or defended by a married person for the immediate benefit of his spouse or of himself and his spouse.

§ 980. Privilege for confidential marital communications

Subject to Section 912 and except as otherwise provided in this article, a spouse (or his guardian or conservator when he has a guardian or conservator), whether or not a party, has a privilege during the marital relationship and afterwards to refuse to disclose, and to prevent another from disclosing, a communication if he claims the privilege and the communication was made in confidence between him and the other spouse while they were husband and wife.

§ 981. Crime or fraud

There is no privilege under this article if the communication was made, in whole or in part, to enable or aid anyone to commit or plan to commit a crime or a fraud.

§ 982. Commitment or similar proceeding

There is no privilege under this article in a proceeding to commit either spouse or otherwise place him or his property, or both, under the control of another because of his alleged mental or physical condition.

§ 983. Proceeding to establish competence

There is no privilege under this article in a proceeding brought by or on behalf of either spouse to establish his competence.

§ 984. Proceeding between spouses

There is no privilege under this article in:

(a) A proceeding brought by or on behalf of one spouse against the other spouse.

(b) A proceeding between a surviving spouse and a person who claims through the deceased spouse, regardless of whether such claim is by testate or intestate succession or by inter vivos transaction.

§ 985. Certain criminal proceedings

There is no privilege under this article in a criminal proceeding in which one spouse is charged with:

(a) A crime committed at any time against the person or property of the other spouse or of a child of either.

(b) A crime committed at any time against the person or property of a third person committed in the course of committing a crime against the person or property of the other spouse.

(c) Bigamy.
(d) A crime defined by Section 270 or 270a of the Penal Code.

APPENDIX E

THE CALIFORNIA INSURANCE EQUITY ACT

Assembly Bill No. 2208
CHAPTER 488

INTRODUCED BY Assembly Member Kehoe
(Principal coauthors: Assembly Members Koretz and Lieber)
(Coauthors: Assembly Members Dymally, Goldberg, Laird, Leno, Levine, Nation, Ridley-Thomas, and Wolk)
(Coauthors: Senators Kuehl, Romero, Soto, Speier, and Vasconcellos)

FEBRUARY 18, 2004

An act to amend Section 1374.58 of the Health and Safety Code, and to amend Section 10121.7 of, and to add Section 381.5 to, the Insurance Code, relating to domestic partners.

LEGISLATIVE COUNSEL'S DIGEST
AB 2208, Kehoe. Health care and insurance benefits.

Existing law, the Knox-Keene Health Care Service Plan Act of 1975, provides for the licensure and regulation of health care service plans and makes a violation of the act's provisions a crime. Existing law also provides for the regulation of health insurers and all other forms of insurance by the Department of Insurance. Under existing law, health care service plans and health insurers are required to offer coverage for the domestic partner of an employee, subscriber, insured, or policyholder to the same extent and subject to the same terms and conditions as provided to a dependent of those persons.

This bill would require a health care service plan and a health insurer to provide coverage to the registered domestic partner of an employee, subscriber, insured, or policyholder that is equal to the coverage it provides to the spouse of those persons. The bill would extend this requirement to all other forms of insurance regulated by the Department of Insurance and would deem that all of those policies as well as health care service plans and health insurance policies issued, amended, delivered, or renewed in this state on or after January 1, 2005, or January 2, 2005, as specified, provide registered domestic partner coverage equal to that provided to spouses. Because the bill would specify additional requirements for a health care service plan, the violation of which would be a crime, it would impose a state-mandated local program.

The California Constitution requires the state to reimburse local agencies and school districts for certain costs mandated by the state. Statutory provisions establish procedures for making that reimbursement.

This bill would provide that no reimbursement is required by this act for a specified reason.

The People of the State of California do enact as follows:

SECTION 1. This act shall be known and may be cited as the California Insurance Equality Act.

SEC. 2. Section 1374.58 of the Health and Safety Code is amended to read:

1374.58. (a) A group health care service plan that provides hospital, medical, or surgical expense benefits shall provide equal coverage to employers or guaranteed associations, as defined in Section 1357, for the registered domestic partner of an employee or subscriber to the same extent, and subject to the same terms and conditions, as provided to a spouse of the employee or subscriber, and shall inform employers and guaranteed associations of this coverage. A plan may not offer or provide coverage for a registered domestic partner that is not equal to the coverage provided to the spouse of an employee or subscriber.

(b) If an employer or guaranteed association has purchased coverage for spouses and registered domestic partners pursuant to subdivision (a), a health care service plan that provides hospital, medical, or surgical expense benefits for employees or subscribers and their spouses shall enroll, upon application by the employer or group administrator, a registered domestic partner of an employee or subscriber in accordance with the terms and conditions of the group contract that apply generally to all spouses under the plan, including coordination of benefits.

(c) For purposes of this section, the term "domestic partner" shall have the same meaning as that term is used in Section 297 of the Family Code.

(d) (1) A health care service plan may require that the employee or subscriber verify the status of the domestic partnership by providing to the plan a copy of a valid Declaration of Domestic Partnership filed with the Secretary of State pursuant to Section 298 of the Family Code or an equivalent document issued by a local agency of this state, another state, or a local agency of another state under which the partnership was created. The plan may also require that the employee or subscriber notify the plan upon the termination of the domestic partnership.
(2) Notwithstanding paragraph (1), a health care service plan may require the information described in that paragraph only if it also requests from the employee or subscriber whose spouse is provided coverage, verification of marital status and notification of dissolution of the marriage.
(e) Nothing in this section shall be construed to expand the requirements of Section 4980B of Title 26 of the United States Code, Section 1161, and following, of Title 29 of the United States Code, or Section 300bb-1, and following, of Title 42 of the United States Code, as added by the Consolidated Omnibus Budget Reconciliation Act of 1985 (Public Law 99-272), and as those provisions may be later amended.
(f) A plan subject to this section that is issued, amended, delivered, or renewed in this state on or after January 2, 2005, shall be deemed to provide coverage for registered domestic partners that is equal to the coverage provided to a spouse of an employee or subscriber.

SEC. 3. Section 381.5 is added to the Insurance Code, to read:
381.5. (a) Every policy issued, amended, delivered, or renewed in this state shall provide coverage for the registered domestic partner of an insured or policyholder that is equal to, and subject to the same terms and conditions as, the coverage provided to a spouse of an insured or policyholder. A policy may not offer or provide coverage for a registered domestic partner if it is not equal to the coverage provided for the spouse of an insured or policyholder. This subdivision applies to all forms of insurance regulated by this code.
(b) A policy subject to this section that is issued, amended, delivered, or renewed in this state on or after January 1, 2005, shall be deemed to provide coverage for registered domestic partners that is equal to the coverage provided to a spouse of an insured or policyholder.
(c) It is the intent of the Legislature that, for purposes of this section, "terms," "conditions," and "coverage" do not include instances of differential treatment of domestic partners and spouses under federal law.

SEC. 4. Section 10121.7 of the Insurance Code is amended to read:
10121.7. (a) A policy of group health insurance that provides hospital, medical, or surgical expense benefits shall provide equal coverage to employers or guaranteed associations, as defined in Section 10700, for the registered domestic partner of an employee, insured, or policyholder to the same extent, and subject to the same terms and conditions, as provided to a spouse of the employee, insured, or policyholder, and shall inform employers and guaranteed associations of this coverage. A policy may not offer or provide coverage for a registered domestic partner that is not equal to the coverage provided to the spouse of an employee, insured, or policyholder.
(b) If an employer or guaranteed association has purchased coverage for spouses and registered domestic partners pursuant to subdivision (a), a health insurer that provides hospital, medical, or surgical expense benefits for employees, insureds, or policyholders and their spouses shall enroll, upon application by the employer or group administrator, a registered domestic partner of the employee, insured, or policyholder in accordance with the terms and conditions of the group contract that apply generally to all spouses under the policy, including coordination of benefits.
(c) For purposes of this section, the term "domestic partner" shall have the same meaning as that term is used in Section 297 of the Family Code.
(d) (1) A policy of group health insurance may require that the employee, insured, or policyholder verify the status of the domestic partnership by providing to the insurer a copy of a valid Declaration of Domestic Partnership filed with the Secretary of State pursuant to Section 298 of the Family Code or an equivalent document issued by a local agency of this state, another state, or a local agency of another state under which the partnership was created. The policy may also require that the employee, insured, or policyholder notify the insurer upon the termination of the domestic partnership.
(2) Notwithstanding paragraph (1), a policy may require the information described in that paragraph only if it also requests from the employee, insured, or policyholder whose spouse is provided coverage, verification of marital status and notification of dissolution of the marriage.
(e) Nothing in this section shall be construed to expand the requirements of Section 4980B of Title 26 of the United States Code, Section 1161, and following, of Title 29 of the United States Code, or Section 300bb-1, and following, of Title 42 of the United States Code, as added by the

Consolidated Omnibus Budget Reconciliation Act of 1985 (Public Law 99-272), and as those provisions may be later amended.

(f) A group health insurance policy subject to this section that is issued, amended, delivered, or renewed in this state on or after January 2, 2005, shall be deemed to provide coverage for registered domestic partners that is equal to the coverage provided to a spouse of an employee, insured, or policyholder.

SEC. 5. No reimbursement is required by this act pursuant to Section 6 of Article XIII B of the California Constitution because the only costs that may be incurred by a local agency or school district will be incurred because this act creates a new crime or infraction, eliminates a crime or infraction, or changes the penalty for a crime or infraction, within the meaning of Section 17556 of the Government Code, or changes the definition of a crime within the meaning of Section 6 of Article XIII B of the California Constitution.

APPENDIX F

SAMPLE TERMINATION AGREEMENT[1]

AGREEMENT TO TERMINATE DOMESTIC PARTNERSHIP

[Name A] and [Name B] registered as domestic partners on [date].

Our domestic partnership can be terminated using the summary termination process because we meet all of the requirements.

1. As of the date of filing the Notice of Termination of Domestic Partnership, it will have been less than five years since we registered as domestic partners. We both have signed the Notice of Termination of Domestic Partnership.
2. There are no children from our relationship born either before or after registration of our domestic partnership or adopted by either or both of us after registration of our domestic partnership. [Lesbian couples should add: Neither of us, to our knowledge, is pregnant.]
3. Neither of us has any interest in real property. Neither of us has a lease for a residence that will last more than one year from the date of filing the Notice of Termination. If we do have a residential lease for less than one year, it does not include a purchase option.
4. The debts we have incurred after the date of registration do not exceed [this amount changes periodically but is currently $4,000]. The debts will be shared in the following manner:

   A's list of debts

   B's list of debts

---

[1] This form is only a sample. This is not intended to be legal advice or representation. The dollar limits change, and you should seek up-to-date information and advice about using this process.

5. The total fair market value of our community property, not including the value of automobiles or of encumbrances on the property, and including deferred compensation and retirement benefits, is not greater than [this amount changes periodically but is currently $32,000]. We have agreed to divide the community property as follows:
   List of community property A receives
   List of community property B receives
6. The total fair market value of the separate property of each of us, not including the value of automobiles or of encumbrances on the property, and including deferred compensation and retirement benefits is not greater than [this amount changes periodically but is currently $32,000].
   List of A's separate property
   List of B's separate property
7. We have either already signed all documents, title certificates, bills of sale, or other evidence of transfer necessary to divide our property and debts or we each agree that we will promptly sign such documents when requested to do so by the other partner.
8. We each agree to waive any claim of spousal support from the other partner. We each understand that once we have waived this right, and our termination is final, we cannot change our mind and make a request for spousal support, even if our circumstances have changed. We each know that we have the right to get advice from an attorney about spousal support. Knowing these things, we each agree to permanently waive the claim of spousal support from our partner.
9. We each agree that we have read the brochure provided by the Secretary of State regarding termination of domestic partnerships and understand the contents of the brochure.
10. We both want to terminate our domestic partnership.

Date signed: ________________ [Signature of Partner A]

Date signed: ________________ [Signature of Partner B]

APPENDIX G

FAMILY CODE

DIVISION 4. Rights and Obligations During Marriage

PART 5. Marital Agreements

CHAPTER 2. **Uniform Premarital Agreement Act**

§1600
This chapter may be cited as the Uniform Premarital Agreement Act.

§1601
This chapter is effective on and after January 1, 1986, and applies to any premarital agreement executed on or after that date.

§1610
As used in this chapter:
(a) "Premarital agreement" means an agreement between prospective spouses made in contemplation of marriage and to be effective upon marriage.
(b) "Property" means an interest, present or future, legal or equitable, vested or contingent, in real or personal property, including income and earnings.

§1611
A premarital agreement shall be in writing and signed by both parties. It is enforceable without consideration.

§1612
(a) Parties to a premarital agreement may contract with respect to all of the following:
(1) The rights and obligations of each of the parties in any of the property of either or both of them whenever and wherever acquired or located.
(2) The right to buy, sell, use, transfer, exchange, abandon, lease, consume, expend, assign, create a security interest in, mortgage,

encumber, dispose of, or otherwise manage and control property.
(3) The disposition of property upon separation, marital dissolution, death, or the occurrence or nonoccurrence of any other event.
(4) The making of a will, trust, or other arrangement to carry out the provisions of the agreement.
(5) The ownership rights in and disposition of the death benefit from a life insurance policy.
(6) The choice of law governing the construction of the agreement.
(7) Any other matter, including their personal rights and obligations, not in violation of public policy or a statute imposing a criminal penalty.
(b) The right of a child to support may not be adversely affected by a premarital agreement.
(c) Any provision in a premarital agreement regarding spousal support, including, but not limited to, a waiver of it, is not enforceable if the party against whom enforcement of the spousal support provision is sought was not represented by independent counsel at the time the agreement containing the provision was signed, or if the provision regarding spousal support is unconscionable at the time of enforcement. An otherwise unenforceable provision in a premarital agreement regarding spousal support may not become enforceable solely because the party against whom enforcement is sought was represented by independent counsel.

§1613
A premarital agreement becomes effective upon marriage.
[NOTE: AB 2580 gives domestic partners until June 30, 2004 to enter into an agreement even if they have already registered as domestic partners.]

§1614
After marriage, a premarital agreement may be amended or revoked only by a written agreement signed by the parties. The amended agreement or the revocation is enforceable without consideration.

§1615
(a) A premarital agreement is not enforceable if the party against whom enforcement is sought proves either of the following:
(1) That party did not execute the agreement voluntarily.
(2) The agreement was unconscionable when it was executed and,

before execution of the agreement, all of the following applied to that party:

(A) That party was not provided a fair, reasonable, and full disclosure of the property or financial obligations of the other party.

(B) That party did not voluntarily and expressly waive, in writing, any right to disclosure of the property or financial obligations of the other party beyond the disclosure provided.

(C) That party did not have, or reasonably could not have had, an adequate knowledge of the property or financial obligations of the other party.

(b) An issue of unconscionability of a premarital agreement shall be decided by the court as a matter of law.

(c) For the purposes of subdivision (a), it shall be deemed that a premarital agreement was not executed voluntarily unless the court finds in writing or on the record all of the following:

(1) The party against whom enforcement is sought was represented by independent legal counsel at the time of signing the agreement or, after being advised to seek independent legal counsel, expressly waived, in a separate writing, representation by independent legal counsel.

(2) The party against whom enforcement is sought had not less than seven calendar days between the time that party was first presented with the agreement and advised to seek independent legal counsel and the time the agreement was signed.

(3) The party against whom enforcement is sought, if unrepresented by legal counsel, was fully informed of the terms and basic effect of the agreement as well as the rights and obligations he or she was giving up by signing the agreement, and was proficient in the language in which the explanation of the party's rights was conducted and in which the agreement was written. The explanation of the rights and obligations relinquished shall be memorialized in writing and delivered to the party prior to signing the agreement. The unrepresented party shall, on or before the signing of the premarital agreement, execute a document declaring that he or she received the information required by this paragraph and indicating who provided that information.

(4) The agreement and the writings executed pursuant to paragraphs (1) and (3) were not executed under duress, fraud, or undue influence, and the parties did not lack capacity to enter into the agreement.

(5) Any other factors the court deems relevant.

§1616
If a marriage is determined to be void, an agreement that would otherwise have been a premarital agreement is enforceable only to the extent necessary to avoid an inequitable result.

§1617
Any statute of limitations applicable to an action asserting a claim for relief under a premarital agreement is tolled during the marriage of the parties to the agreement. However, equitable defenses limiting the time for enforcement, including laches and estoppel, are available to either party.

APPENDIX H

FAMILY CODE
DIVISION 9. Support
PART 2. Child Support
CHAPTER 2. Court-Ordered Child Support
ARTICLE 2. **Statewide Uniform Guideline**

§ 4055. Formula for statewide uniform guideline for determining child support

(a) The statewide uniform guideline for determining child support orders is as follows: CS = K [HN - (H%) (TN)].

(b) (1) The components of the formula are as follows:

(A) CS = child support amount.

(B) K = amount of both parents' income to be allocated for child support as set forth in paragraph (3).

(C) HN = high earner's net monthly disposable income.

(D) H% = approximate percentage of time that the high earner has or will have primary physical responsibility for the children compared to the other parent. In cases in which parents have different time-sharing arrangements for different children, H% equals the average of the approximate percentages of time the high earner parent spends with each child.

(E) TN = total net monthly disposable income of both parties.

(2) To compute net disposable income, see Section 4059.

(3) K (amount of both parents' income allocated for child support) equals one plus H% (if H% is less than or equal to 50 percent) or two minus H% (if H% is greater than 50 percent) times the following fraction:

Total Net Disposable
Income Per Month K
$ 0-800 0.20 + TN/16,000
$ 801-6,666 0.25
$ 6,667-10,000 0.10 + 1,000/TN
Over $ 10,000 0.12 + 800/TN

For example, if H 7.986117e-222quals 20 percent and the total monthly net disposable income of the parents is $ 1,000, K = (1 + 0.20) x 0.25, or 0.30. If H% equals 80 percent and the total monthly net disposable income of the parents is $ 1,000, K = (2 - 0.80) x 0.25, or 0.30.

(4) For more than one child, multiply CS by:

2 children 1.6

3 children 2

4 children 2.3

5 children 2.5

6 children 2.625

7 children 2.75

8 children 2.813

9 children 2.844

10 children 2.86

(5) If the amount calculated under the formula results in a positive number, the higher earner shall pay that amount to the lower earner. If the amount calculated under the formula results in a negative number, the lower earner shall pay the absolute value of that amount to the higher earner.

(6) In any default proceeding where proof is by affidavit pursuant to Section 2336, or in any proceeding for child support in which a party fails to appear after being duly noticed, H% shall be set at zero in the formula if the noncustodial parent is the higher earner or at 100 if the custodial parent is the higher earner, where there is no evidence presented demonstrating the percentage of time that the noncustodial parent has primary physical responsibility for the children. H% shall not be set as described above if the moving party in a default proceeding is the noncustodial parent or if the party who fails to appear after being duly noticed is the custodial parent. A statement by the party who is not in default as to the percentage of time that the noncustodial parent has primary physical responsibility for the children shall be deemed sufficient evidence.

(7) In all cases in which the net disposable income per month of the obligor is less than one thousand dollars ($ 1,000), there shall be a rebuttable presumption that the obligor is entitled to a low-income adjustment . The presumption may be rebutted by evidence showing that the application of the low-income adjustment would be unjust and inappropriate in the particular case. In determining whether the

presumption is rebutted, the court shall consider the principles provided in Section 4053, and the impact of the contemplated adjustment on the respective net incomes of the obligor and the obligee. The low-income adjustment shallreduce the child support amount otherwise determined under this section by an amount that is no greater than the amount calculated by multiplying the child support amount otherwise determined under this section by a fraction, the numerator of which is 1,000 minus the obligor's net disposable income per month, and the denominator of which is 1,000.

(8) Unless the court orders otherwise, the order for child support shall allocate the support amount so that the amount of support for the youngest child is the amount of support for one child, and the amount for the next youngest child is the difference between that amount and the amount for two children, with similar allocations for additional children. However, this paragraph does not apply to cases in which there are different time-sharing arrangements for different children or where the court determines that the allocation would be inappropriate in the particular case.

(c) If a court uses a computer to calculate the child support order, the computer program shall not automatically default affirmatively or negatively on whether a low-income adjustment is to be applied. If the low-income adjustment is applied, the computer program shall not provide the amount of the low-income adjustment. Instead, the computer program shall ask the user whether or not to apply the low-income adjustment, and if answered affirmatively, the computer program shall provide the range of the adjustment permitted by paragraph (7) of subdivision (b).

INDEX